D0759753

CIVIC CENTER

The Freshwater Angler™

COMPLETE PHOTO GUIDE TO
FLY FISHING
300 Strategies, Techniques and Insights

C. Boyd Pfeiffer

Creative Publishing
international

Chanhassen, Minnesota

C. Boyd Pfeiffer, an award-winning outdoor journalist and photographer, has been published in more than 70 magazines, including *Saltwater Fly Fishing, Outdoor Life, American Angler*. He has authored 23 books on fishing and outdoor photography. He lives in Phoenix, Maryland.

Creative Publishing
international

Copyright © 2006 by Creative Publishing international, Inc.
18705 Lake Drive East
Chanhassen, MN 55317
1-800-328-3895
www.creativepub.com
All rights reserved.

President/CEO: Ken Fund
Vice President/Publisher: Linda Ball
Vice President/Retail Sales & Marketing: Kevin Haas
Executive Editor, Outdoor Group: Barbara Harold
Creative Director: Brad Springer
Book Designer: Kari Johnston
Project Manager: Tracy Stanley
Production Manager: Laura Hokkanen
Production Staff: Helga Thielen

Printed in China
10 9 8 7 6 5 4 3 2 1

COMPLETE PHOTO GUIDE TO FLY FISHING
by C. Boyd Pfeiffer

All photographs copyright © 2006 C. Boyd Pfeiffer except:
Front cover (top) by West Virginia Division of Tourism—Steve Shaluta/WV Tourism; p. 20, 23, 24, 57, 58 (top), 67 (top), 74, 75 (both), 78, 88 (top), 101 (center) by Brenda Pfeiffer; p.3, 5, 12, 28, 54, 70, 80, 108, 114 © 2006 by Creative Publishing international, Inc.

NOTE: For visual clarity, some photos may show flies larger than normal or line/leaders that are thicker diameter than normal and/or artificially colored.

Angler quotations reproduced with permission from *The Quotable Fisherman* by Nick Lyons, The Lyons Press, ©1998.

To Brenda

ACKNOWLEDGMENTS

From the time we first pick up a fly rod, we are learning tips and tricks. Initially they are simple tips—double the line when you thread it through the guides, don't put your reel on backward, learn the right knots, attach backing to the fly line securely, clean your fly tackle, learn the basic fly casts, set your drag properly, etc., etc., etc. In time we learn more tips, but we are always learning. Sometimes it is hard to remember who taught us what tip, but there are always those interested in sharing their knowledge and experience with us, explaining shortcuts, describing better techniques, and making fly fishing easier and, thus, more fun.

Over the years, I have learned a lot from many fly fishermen, ofttimes those met along a streambank. Or I have picked up a trick from someone when fishing in a tropical flats boat, wading a stream, or sharing experiences about the best bass bug for certain waters. I have read about a new fly fishing wrinkle in a magazine article or book. I have learned from those met at fly and tackle shows, those with whom I have fished on a trip, and those giving tips at a fishing club meeting.

I find that both close friends (whom I count among some top experts) and longtime acquaintances are willing—even anxious—to share their knowledge and experience. These include people such as Lefty Kreh, Chuck Edghill, Ed Russell, Norm Bartlett, Bill May, Jim Heim, Gary Neitzey, Joe Zimmer, George Reiger, Irv Swope, Jack Goellner, and so many others. To all of these fly anglers—close buddies and casual acquaintances—along with those I may have forgotten with a memory dimmed by the years—I say thank you.

My special thanks go to Chuck Edghill, a longtime friend who has, with this and previous books, kindly taken on the onerous task of reading the manuscript as a second check before it goes to the publisher. Chuck is expert in freshwater and saltwater fishing, and fly fishing. He's also an accomplished and former commercial flytier and an excellent editor who used to write and edit blast furnace operations manuals for Bethlehem Steel. In addition, Chuck helped with the photos, posing for hours on the water for specific photos to illustrate various tips. Chuck—my thanks—this book is better because of your efforts, kindness, and experience, and my many mistakes you caught. Any remaining mistakes are, of course, mine alone.

My thanks also to Barbara Harold, my editor at Creative Publishing, who first saw the value of such a book and saw it through to the end. Thank you to Brenda, my wife, who photographed specific shots for the book. She also gave me the time for this project and encouraged me with this, as she does with all of my efforts, and indeed with life.

Library of Congress Cataloging-in-Publication Data

Pfeiffer, C. Boyd.
  Complete photo guide to fly fishing : 300 strategies, techniques and insights / C. Boyd Pfeiffer.
      p. cm.
  Includes index.
  ISBN 1-58923-220-8 (hard cover)
  1. Fly fishing. 2. Fly fishing—Pictorial works. I. Title.
  SH456.P49 2005
  799.12'4—dc22
                                    2005002681

TABLE OF CONTENTS

Introduction

ook up the word "tip" in the dictionary, and among the many definitions you will find that a tip is a piece of information, a suggestion, a hint, or such, sometimes given secretly, as if it is confidential or special. In the case of fly anglers, tips and tricks are those little tidbits of information that lead to a simpler, better, faster, cheaper, more effective, more organized, or more efficient way of doing something connected with fly fishing. That "something" might be dealing with tackle, rigging your fly outfit, fighting a fish, landing a fish, casting under difficult conditions, cleaning your gear, fly fishing from boats, solving stream fly fishing problems, releasing fish, unsnagging flies, etc.

In all cases, it is something distinct and well defined. A long dissertation on how to fight a fish with a fly rod is not a tip. Using side pressure to turn a fish in order to lessen the possibility of it becoming unbuttoned is a tip. Worrying about fly line blowing around a boat deck is not a tip. Using a mesh-side laundry hamper as a stripping basket is a tip. Describing how to repair a rod that was broken by running the tip section into a tree when walking the streambank is only an after-the-fact regret. Suggesting that you carry the rod butt first to prevent this sad situation is a tip.

Here are 300 of these tips on all aspects of freshwater and saltwater fishing, boat fly fishing, gear, care of flies and tackle, protecting yourself from the elements, traveling with fly tackle, using lines and leaders, fly storage, and so on, to help you get more out of our sport of fly fishing.

I've divided the tips into sections so that you can go to a specific concern and find an answer to a vexing problem. In some cases, there might be only one solution—or one solution presented here and the only one that I know—to solve a specific problem. In

other cases, you might have several choices from which to pick the tip or solution best suited to your fly fishing. You might find some old standards here, but you will also find some new tips, which hopefully will help you get more fun out of fly fishing.

When I learn new tips and tricks, I try them to prove (or sometimes disprove) their efficacy. Those that don't work, I discard. And what I do learn in tips, tricks, wrinkles, and methods of doing something, I try to pass along. This, then, is a gathering of those tips, some developed by me, but many learned from others and some just common sense. This is an effort to share these ideas more widely to make the sport of fly fishing a little more fun and a little less work. Enjoy, learn, experience—and pass along your knowledge to others.

Chapter 1

Fly Fishing Myths
Settling a Few Debates

1 WEIGHT-FORWARD VERSUS DOUBLE-TAPER LINES

The argument used to be (and sometimes still is) that a double-taper line provides a more delicate presentation of the fly than any of the weight-forward lines. This is not true, although there are a few exceptions. Manufacturers base presentation on the degree or length of the front taper of the line, from the belly to the very short level section at the end. Line manufacturers debate this, citing mass/air-resistance ratios, floating versus sinking lines and their respective diameters, etc, but it basically comes down to front taper length. Many weight-forward lines available today have a front taper that is as long as or longer than that of most double-tapers.

There are exceptions, with the so-called "bass bug tapers" usually having a shorter front taper than that of double-tapers. But with that exception, most weight-forward tapers give you as, or more, delicate a presentation than double-tapers, along with the advantage of the front-weighted belly that makes them easier for distance casting.

The main advantage of a double taper is that you can reverse it when the one end wears out to get double the fishing time from one line. If you never cast long distances, consider this. Otherwise, opt for a weight-forward taper after checking the specs of the respective front tapers of the line brand you choose to make sure that you are getting the line that performs best for your fishing.

2 ROD GRIP

When buying a fly rod, make sure that the grip is comfortable. If you want a certain brand of rod, you may not have a choice, but if you are open to several brands, there are options. While cigar-shaped grips are popular for most small rods, some rod companies use a Half Wells grip, with the Half Wells put on in reverse so that the thin tapered end is at the front. This makes the rod more aesthetically pleasing, but far less functional. And form should follow function.

Many rod manufacturers use the same reversed Half Wells on larger rods. This is wrong, since anything over a size 6-weight rod, or any rod that you use for long casts, should have a Half Wells put on correctly (swelled end at the front) or fitted with a Full Wells (swollen at both ends). This swollen end makes a good thumb rest and makes it easier to punch out a long cast than with a cigar grip, reversed Half Wells, or other slim grip.

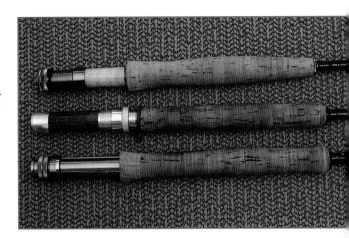

3 RIGHT- OR LEFT-HAND RETRIEVE

Anglers debate about whether to rig reels to retrieve line with the casting hand or the opposing line hand. If you are not after big fish, it doesn't matter much, provided that you are happy with your rig. Many experts agree that if you are after big fish that run out a lot of line or you are making long casts that require frequent lengthy reel retrieves, it is best to have the reel handle on the "rod casting" side. Thus, for big fish, always set up your reels so that you switch hands to fight the fish and retrieve with the dominant (casting) hand.

Reasons for this include: your dominant hand has more strength for long retrieves; your dominant hand can retrieve in small circles (spinning, with which this is often compared, requires large hand-turning circles); and your dominant hand has finer control if you must use a palming technique to exert drag pressure on the reel. Remember to fish the system with which you are most comfortable.

4 DIRECT-DRIVE VERSUS ANTI-REVERSE REELS

Fly reels come in two basic styles, direct-drive (left) and anti-reverse (right) models. Direct-drive models are just that—the handle is attached to the spool so that turning the handle turns the spool. There is no slippage, no braking action, and no drag as long as you have your hand on the reel handle. Anti-reverse reels have a separate plate or bar to which the handle is attached. The spool slips with the drag setting of the reel when a fish takes line, without the handle turning or moving backward.

Most freshwater and light-tackle inshore anglers use direct-drive reels while some offshore anglers like anti-reverse reels. But reel choice is not that simple. For example, if using a reel set with a very light drag while using a very light tippet, the anti-reverse reel has minimal advantage, since it is easily possible to turn the reel handle as the drag slips without moving or tiring the fish. Thus, the anti-reverse reels are best when using stouter tippets (big game fishing) and heavy drag settings that allow reeling in line when you turn the handle.

If you can't reel in line, the heavier force required to reel alerts you to this. Direct drive is best for light tippets, but has the disadvantage of the reel handles spinning anytime a big fish takes line. Thus, you have to release the handle on a direct-drive reel when a strong fish takes line or risk a break-off and/or hand injury.

5 WEIGHTED FLIES

For some fishing, weighted flies are a must. This includes steelhead fishing, fishing for Pacific salmon, and some warm-water fishing such as that for largemouth, smallmouth, and pike. Where possible, avoid tying or fishing with heavily weighted flies. The heavy weight does have the advantage of getting the fly down to the fish, but has the disadvantage of deadening the action and movement of any fly. The heavy dumbbell eye weights in a fly can also cause the hook to ride point up, an advantage in preventing snags when fishing the bottom.

As an alternative, tie flies without weight or with very little weight, and use other weighting methods to get the fly deep. Possibilities for this include using several split shot on a leader, using a sinking or sinking-tip line, or using a "mini lead head" of several feet of lead-core line in the middle of the leader or between the line and a short leader. You can buy these mini lead heads (Gudebrod, Orvis, and Cortland) or make your own from 2-foot (0.6-m) lengths of lead-core line with loops spliced and wrapped into each end for loop-to-loop connections with the leader/line. If so inclined or required in your fishing area, you can also use non-lead weighted line.

"No angler merely watches nature in a passive way. He enters into its very existence."

—John Bailey
Reflections on the Water's Edge (N.D.)

6 LEVEL LEADERS

There used to be many different variations and formulas for leaders for different species, different rod weights, and different fishing situations. Today, we can fish efficiently with one leader formula for most fishing situations, only varying the length, tippet length, and tippet strength.

But if you are out of leader material temporarily, you can still do a lot of fishing with a level leader. This is nothing more than a length of mono that is your tippet size, tied with a loop at one end to connect to your fly line. Admittedly, such leaders cause a slight hinge effect when casting and you must replace the leader when any part of it abrades. (Abrasion on tapered leaders above the tippet has little weakening effect on the whole leader.) But level leaders do work. They are best when used in about the 10- to 15-pound-test (4.5- to 6.8-kg) range, which suggests their use for heavy trout, bass, saltwater inshore fishing, and pike (with a wire bite leader added for pike). They are best when fished with heavier outfits, using short leaders and fishing small flies. They are not as good with flies that have a high ratio of air resistance to mass, which tends to slow the turnover of even the best leaders. Use a level leader if you get into an emergency.

7 FLUOROCARBON LEADERS AND TIPPETS

Fluorocarbon line and tippet material for fly fishing has had a lot of "advantages" ascribed to it, but much is hype. The proponents of the material point to the fact that when compared to monofilament, it is less visible in the water, has more abrasion resistance, does not weaken by absorbing water, sinks faster, and is stiffer. All this is true, but at some cost and with other factors that you should consider. For example, while it is less visible in the water, it is only by a slight amount. Water has an average refractive index of 1.33. (Light, water pressure, and temperature can slightly affect this index.) The refractive index for nylon monofilament is about 1.52, while the refractive index for fluorocarbon tippets is 1.42.

Thus, while fluorocarbon is less visible than monofilament in the water, it also has a lower tensile strength for a given diameter. To get the same tensile strength as mono, you must use a larger-diameter fluorocarbon tippet, thus negating some of the supposed advantages of the reduced visibility. It does have much better abrasion resistance than mono, but against this is the fact that it is also stiffer, thus reducing the action of any fly in the water. It does not absorb water. Mono does absorb water, becoming slightly weaker as a result.

Fluorocarbon sinks faster than mono—about 3 to 4 inches (7.6 to 10.2 cm) per second as opposed to about 1 inch (2.5 cm) per second with mono, but this can be a plus or a minus, depending upon the fishing situation. If lost as litter, fluorocarbon does not break down with time. Mono slowly becomes brittle and breaks down, thus reducing the danger to wildlife. Finally, the cost is about ten times that of premium mono.

8 LEADER LENGTH FOR SINKING LINES

Most leaders come in lengths from about 7 1/2 to 12 feet (2.3 to 3.7 m). However, if fishing deep with sinking or sinking-tip lines, these are entirely too long. Too long a leader bellies up in the water if you have a sinking line and a sinking fly, or causes a non-sinking fly to suspend high in the water column without ever getting deep.

To solve this, make your leader for a sinking line no more than 3 feet (0.9 m) long. Consider a 1-foot (0.3-m) length of heavy butt section and a 2-foot (0.6-m) length of the required tippet size. The butt section might have to be of lower test strength than normally used to be able to easily tie knots to connect the two leader lengths.

9 FROM LEFTY KREH...

Joe Brooks, well-known outdoor writer and mentor, introduced me to fly fishing in 1947. I became immediately addicted to it. In the nearly 60 years since that time I have been lucky enough to fish over much of the planet in both fresh and saltwater.

There are many things that keep fly fishing as fresh in my heart and mind as in 1947. I think the most important is that I continually keep learning. An example I often cite to young outdoor writers concerns a young man at a California fishing clinic. During the 1950s I became interested in knots and over several years a huge amount of data was amassed. Using this information with Mark Sosin we co-authored a book published in the early 1970s that is still in print.

Our publisher, Nick Lyons, insisted that we only include 40 knots, but they had to cover everything from using cable for offshore billfishing to tying with an 8X tippet. Over the next ten years or so after the book came out scores of people showed me knots that weren't in the book. I was force fed the information and knew as many knots as almost anyone.

During a clinic in California I demonstrated nine ways to attach a leader to a fly line. Each took several minutes to tie. I asked if there were any questions and a young man raised his hand. "Yes, son, what is it?" He answered, "I think I have a better way." I said, "Well, get up here and show us."

The lad took a needle, a piece of fly line and a leader butt section and in about 12 seconds handed me a perfect nail knot. I turned to the audience and said, "Forget what this expert showed you and let's find out what this young man did."

It was there that I learned to tie the speedy nail knot, which I have shared with many others. The important point to be made is a near-world expert on a subject can learn something from even a 12-year-old boy.

That is just one reason I love the sport of fly fishing.

"Quite possibly this is the key to fishing: the ability to see glamour in whatever species one may fish for."

—Harold Blaisdell
The Philisophical Fisherman

10 STUFF THAT IS BAD FOR YOUR FLY LINE

We all know that monofilament is impervious to almost any-thing, except battery acid. Long exposure to sun and heat also degrades it. Avoid products that can impart a scent to the line. (A possible exception is WD-40, which some anglers use to spray lures and baits, stating that it attracts fish.) But fly lines are different in that they are made (most of them, anyway) of a PVC coating over a mono or braided core. The PVC coating is susceptible to some degree of damage from a number of things, including a long list of outdoor and personal products, such as DEET insect repellent, some perfumes, sunscreens, oil, gasoline, fly sinks and floats, alcohol-based products, and petroleum-based demoisturizing agents, such as WD-40.

This last one has always loomed large on the radar screen of fly fishermen, since it seems to make it impossible to spray your reel with this protective petrole-um product without hitting the fly line, unless the fly line is removed. Anglers name WD-40 as particularly bad for fly lines—some even suggest it will dis-solve lines in short order.

11 CONVENTIONAL VERSUS LARGE-ARBOR REELS

Large-arbor reels are sometimes rated as "better" than conventional reels in that they supposedly retrieve more line with each turn of the han-dle, retrieve line more quickly, reduce stress, reduce fatigue when reeling, etc. That is true if you are choosing a large-arbor reel that has a larger overall diameter than the reel that you would otherwise use. It is not true if you are buying a large-arbor reel that is the same or very close to the diameter of the conventional reel you are replacing. "Pi" in physics remains constant, and a large-arbor reel of the same diameter as a conventional reel has no advantages. It only becomes a "reduced-line-capacity" reel. Of course, both reels must have the same spool width to make comparisons equal.

12 FOAM FLY BOXES

Many experts agree that foam fly boxes are best for those anglers who do not fish much. This is because putting a fly hook into a foam ridge leaves a permanent hole. Even if you do not remove the flies, the hole in time becomes larger and the fly becomes loose. Repeated removal and return of flies to these boxes only increases the number or size of holes and the possibility of losing flies. One exception is the fly box that has foam cut with slits.

The fly hook is held in the slit between the foam sides (called Micro-slit foam by the companies making them), thus not creating a hole in the foam. These, presently made by C & F and Scientific Anglers, are ideal. Otherwise, stick to compartment boxes (ideal for dries) or the metal clip style of boxes (like Perrine) that hold flies by metal clips. The individual compartment style, such as the Wheatley boxes, and its imitations, are also excellent.

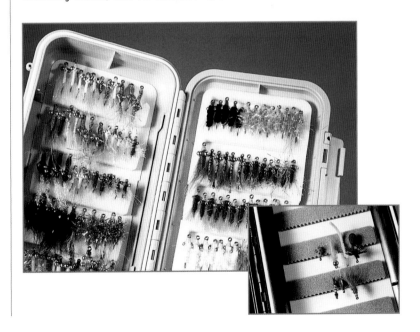

Chapter 2

Getting Ready

Preparing Before Leaving Home

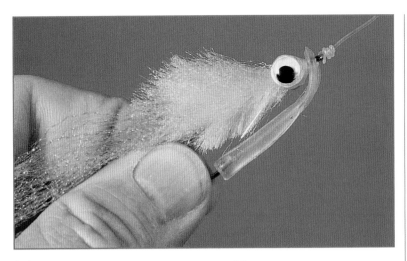

14 WEEDLESS FLIES FOR SNAGS

Weedless flies are not only for weedy situations. They are also great when fishing around snags, through brush piles, over logs, around docks or any other structure that can hang up a fly. The best weed guards on flies are the double-mono-loop style that cover both sides of the hook and protect it even when snaked on its side over a log.

15 CONTROLLING LEADERS AND LINES

You can control coiled leaders and lines and keep them untangled by several means. One way is to use short twist ties, like those used for trash bags. You can also use chenille-type pipe cleaners, cut in half. A third way is to use rubber bands. By looping a rubber band around the coil and then through itself, you can cinch up the rubber band until it is tight and stays tight on the line/leader coil. For best results, secure at three different spots around the perimeter of the coil. It also helps to label the line or leader so that you know what you have when you use it the next time.

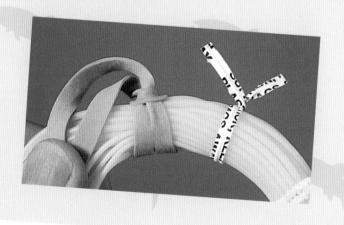

13 ALTERNATIVE WEED GUARD

Unless you tie a fly with a weed guard built in, you can't add one later—unless you are using large flies. Lure anglers use clear, short lengths of soft plastic that are fitted over the eye of a jig and then threaded onto a hook point to protect it.

Do the same thing with flies by threading your fly tippet through the end of the soft plastic weed guard, tying on the fly, and then rigging the weed guard over the fly point. Since these are not small, this is best with streamer or long-shank flies in about size 6 and larger. You can also use them on popping bugs and sliders. These are available from regular tackle shops and catalog houses—not fly shops.

You can do the same thing by dividing or splitting a clear plastic worm lengthwise into four sections, then cutting to length for use as a weed guard. There is no hole through which to thread the leader, so you have to carry a needle to thread the tippet through the end of the weed guard. An easy alternative is to push the head of the fly through the soft plastic and then tie the leader to the fly.

16 DUSK AND NIGHT FISHING

Fishing at night or even dusk is tough when you have to change flies on fine tippets. One way to avoid this problem is to pre-tie tippets to flies that you might use during low-light situations. Then tie a loop knot (perfection loop, surgeon's loop, or figure-eight loop) in the end of each tippet and tie a similar loop in the leader where it attaches to each tippet. Make this loop larger than normal, about 2 inches (5 cm) in size, for easy adding or removal from the loop end leader. Then when you are fishing and can no longer see to tie on flies, it is simple to disconnect the loops and add a new fly by interconnecting the loops without tying.

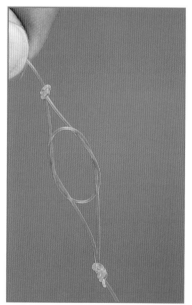

17 RAIN PARKA

It can rain at any time, so always carry a raincoat while fishing. When wading, you have to carry it in the large pocket in back of your fishing vest or chest pack where it can be heavy, bulky, and hot. A simpler method is to carry one of the disposable clear plastic rain parkas that covers completely when wearing chest-high waders and is long enough when wearing hip boots.

Disposable raincoats are inexpensive and available from fly shops, tackle shops, general sporting goods stores, camping supply stores, and many discount stores. They take no more space than a pack of cigarettes, with care can be used a couple of times, and are convenient.

"To me, bream on a fly rod are as pretty fishing as a man can want, but there are times when they aren't worth working for."

—John Graves
Goodbye to a River (1960)

18 USING A GUIDE

Guides are well worth their money and often underpaid for their services. Even if you are an experienced angler, you should consider using a guide under the following circumstances:

• If you are fishing a new area and are completely unfamiliar with the fishing, fish species, water, best flies, and which retrieves to use.

• If you need a boat to fish effectively and do not have one. Fly fishing guides have the right type of boat, complete with casting platforms and other amenities for fly fishing.

• Often guides provide the right type of tackle for the fishing, thus eliminating the need to buy a complete outfit for fishing that you might only do occasionally.

• Guides know where to go and how to fish under any possible situation, thus eliminating wasted time and effort.

• Guides often know about the area, providing a running commentary about birds, wildlife, geology, and history of the area you are fishing.

• Guides know safe wading areas when wade fishing and safe boating areas when boat fishing, thus providing an additional margin of security when fishing new waters.

• When boat fishing, the guide runs the boat, leaving the fishing and relaxing to you and your partner and making for a more pleasurable day.

19 HELPING YOUR GUIDE HELP YOU FISH

Your guide or boat captain wants you to catch fish. You can help. Several guides and captains have suggested the following tips:

• Show up ready to fish. This means with the reel mounted on the rod, line and leader through the guides, and fly tied on.

• Bring rain gear, a hat or cap, and sunscreen, regardless of the weather forecast. You can get sunburned on a cloudy day and rain gear will protect you from boat spray and wind on a bright day.

• Leave all extra stuff at home. This in particular means rod tubes, which are a nuisance at best and a danger at worst on boats.

• Know all the basics and ask questions beforehand. Is the guide/captain providing lunch? When and where will you meet? How long will you fish? What gear will the captain/guide provide (often flies, sometimes complete tackle outfits)?

• Decide if the guide/captain will fish. Some guides/captains expect to fish, some will not fish unless the client suggests it. More bass guides fish than saltwater guides, etc. Sometimes, having a guide or captain fish for a while so that you can get used to the casting targets, how to approach fish, and how to retrieve flies is very useful as a learning experience. Get the basics and understandings established while, or before, booking the trip.

• Be honest with the guide/captain. If you are unsure of your casting skill, knot tying ability, or fish fighting ability, tell the guide/captain. It is far easier to teach you some basics of casting on "dead" water than when trout are rising or stripers breaking along a saltwater jetty. Let the captain/guide know your concerns and weaknesses before you hit the good water.

• Share cell phone and pager numbers with your guide/captain. If some emergency arises while on the way to the meeting spot, you can communicate.

20 THREADING YOUR ROD

Run the line through your fly rod by first doubling the line and using this doubled end to thread each guide. That way, if you slip and drop the line, the doubled end catches in the next guide down so that you do not have to completely rethread the rod. Also, once the doubled end clears the tiptop, flipping the rod will pull out the rest of the line and the leader.

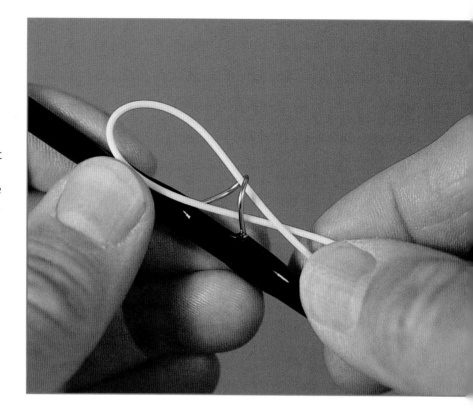

21 PINS IN YOUR FISHING VEST

Stick a few different-size safety pins into your fishing vest. They are handy for clearing the head cement out of flies. Different sizes make this task easy on various-size flies. They are also handy if something breaks on a strap or other part of your gear, to be used for a quick, temporary repair.

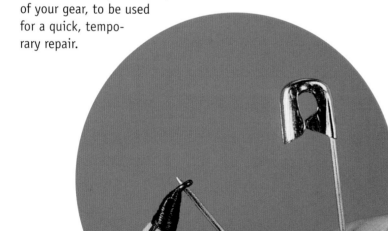

22 KEEP THE SUN AT YOUR BACK

It is not always possible, but if you can keep the sun at your back while fishing, you gain lots of advantages. For one, it is easier to spot fish and water structure than when looking into the sun and trying to see through the glare on the water. In addition, if fish are facing you, they will be facing into the sun, which minimizes and hides any view of you. Third, it minimizes the chance of fish being spooked by the fly line in the air or on the water.

23 REMOVING LEADER COILS

Leaders coil up when stored on the reel or in a leader wallet. To straighten them, pull on the leader material with your hands or let the leader material slide through your hands as you pull on it. Use tension to create friction through your hands so that the slight heat helps straighten the leader. Make sure that you use less pressure as you progress from the heavy butt section to the lighter taper and tippet. Do not use a rubber patch as was done in the past, since this can create enough heat to harm the mono. Some patches of synthetic rubber also soil the mono.

25 CUTTING MONO

An easy way to cut mono leader material is with a nail clipper. To make this simple to use, remove the lever arm and bar from the clipper and use your finger and thumb to press the edges together to cut mono. Strung from a loop of cord, this makes it easy and convenient to cut and adjust leaders and to trim knots. Hang it from a button or "D" ring on your vest.

24 CASE FOR SPARE LINES

Spare lines are easy to install if you use the loop-to-loop connections of line/backing previously described. But you have to carry them some way. The best way is to coil up each line, use a string-tag label to mark the line weight and other characteristics (the marking system described on page 42 for weight and sink rate should suffice), and store them in a case. Try a nylon-fabric CD case, often available on sale for a few bucks from discount stores. Store each line in a separate plastic sleeve. You can carry up to half a dozen lines in one of these cases. If carrying this on the stream, slip it into the rear pocket on your fishing vest.

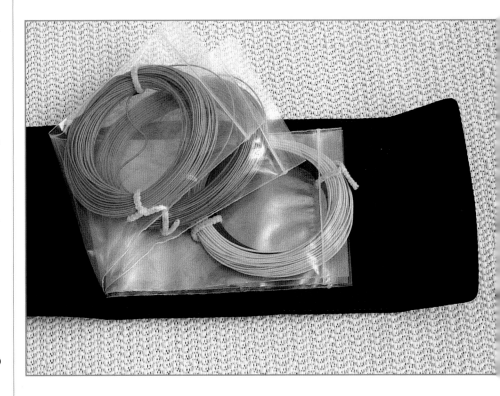

"Many ask, 'Why do you fish?' I've heard the standard answers: 'It's the challenge.' 'It's the wonderful destinations.' 'It's the people you meet.' 'It's the serenity.' I've thought about it a bunch, and for me it's meant many things, over the years, but these days, it's just LEAVING THE DOCK."

—Flip Pallot

26 FIRST AID KIT

Most camping supply stores sell first aid kits. These are no larger than a pack of cigarettes for individual use or large breadbox-size kits for extended use. Make sure that you always have an appropriate-size kit with you on any fishing trip. The smallest kits, containing the bare essentials, easily fit into your pocket. Check the kits before carrying them afield and add anything that you specifically need for your medical needs. Possibilities for additions would be back-up prescription medications, remedies for allergic reactions, and antiseptic for scrapes and hook punctures.

27 SLIP-ON WADER GRIPPERS

Chain or stud types of slip-on rubber grippers are available to fit over waders or hip boots. These are elastic to fit the boot bottom, but with metal studs or cleats to grip the algae-covered rocks. You can use them for both boot-foot and separate wading-boot waders. These are highly recommended for really slippery bottoms, since the studs or chains cut through the scum and algae on rocks and gravel.

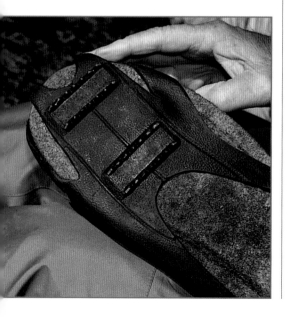

28 MAKE YOUR OWN FIRST AID KIT

You don't have to buy a ready-made first aid kit for your fishing—you can make your own. Fill it from your home medicine cabinet with those items that you need, depending upon the type of kit you are making. You can make a small kit for your fishing vest, a bigger kit for your boat or car, or a large camp-style kit for a number of people over an extended trip. Some possibilities for such kits include, but are not limited to:

• Pocket kit—several sizes of Band-Aids, iodine, aspirin, antacid tablets, alcohol prep pads, loop of heavy cord (for pulling hooks out of flesh), insect bite relief.

• Boat/car kit—all of the above, in larger quantities and variety, plus roll of adhesive tape, packets of sterile dressing pads (several sizes, including 4X4), elastic bandage, gauze roll, sunscreen, sunburn lotion.

• Camp or extended-trip kit—all the above, in larger quantities and varieties, along with roll bandages, triangular bandage, mild soap, blunt-tip scissors, tweezers, eye dropper, eye drops, zipper-seal plastic bags (for ice), disposable single-use ice packs.

In all the above kits, make sure that you include any special medicines or prescriptions for special needs of anyone in the party, such as inhalers for allergic reactions, daily prescription pills if going overnight, etc.

To store the contents, use a small zipper-seal plastic bag, empty candy tin, school soft-side pencil case, utility plastic box, plastic cigarette case, or similar containers. Label the kit with a red or black felt-tip marker.

30 EYEGLASSES

As we get older, many of us have trouble tying small flies to thin tippets, particularly with non-prescription sunglasses or when fishing at dawn or dusk. To solve this, buy some of the clip-on close-up lenses. Gudebrod, for example, makes Fold Away Reading Glasses in eight magnifications from +1.50 to +3.25 for any vision needed. They clip onto any visor or billed cap for easy use in the field, and flip out of the way when not needed.

31 PRESOAK FLIES

Fluffy and wool-material flies are difficult to sink, and often require a couple of casts to soak completely and get down to the fish. There is an easy way to solve this problem. If you know that you are going to fish these flies, carry a small zipper-seal plastic bag, add a little water, and soak the flies. Make sure that once you finish fishing you remove the flies from the bag and allow them to dry thoroughly before returning them to your fly box.

29 REMOVING LINE COILS

Most fly lines retain some coiling when stripped from the reel for casting. This can impede casting, particularly when shooting line for a long cast. To prepare a line for fishing, stretch it to remove any coiling. This is particularly important in cold weather.

To do this, have an angling buddy hold the loop of line while you hold the end and the reel after you spool out a cast-length of line. Have him or her hold the line at this loop while you pull on both ends. Then return the favor for him with his fly line. If by yourself, loop the line around a tree limb, side mirror mount on your car, or similar structure to pull on the line to remove stretch. Just make sure that any structure used does not have any sharp edges, points, or rough spots that can damage the fly line finish. Round posts or tree limbs are best for this. If all else fails, remove large coils and stretch the line gently but firmly between your hands, a 6-foot (1.8-meter) section at a time. Repeat until you have stretched all the castable line and it is straight for casting.

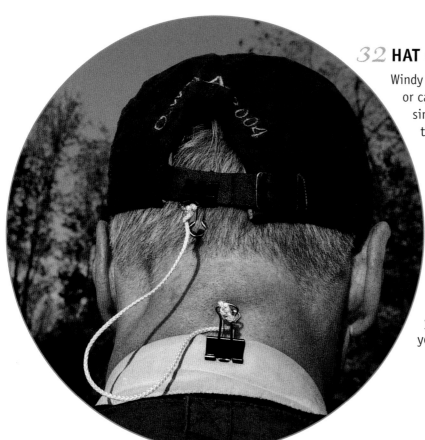

32 HAT CLIPS

Windy situations can cause you to lose a hat or cap in a hurry, and sometimes it will sink before you can get it or can turn the boat around to retrieve it. To prevent this, use a lanyard clip that fastens the back of your hat to the back of your fishing shirt or jacket. If you do not have one or cannot find one, get two spring clips (banker's clips or bulldog clips, available at office supply stores) and tie them to the ends of a shoelace or foot-long (30-cm) cord. Then, when the wind increases, pull the clip out of your fishing vest pocket, and clip to your hat and shirt to prevent loss.

33 SPLIT SHOT AND SMALL SHOT

To use split shot effectively to sink your flies, use several small split shot instead or one or two big split shot. Position the split shot along the leader several inches apart to spread out the weight so that there is less likelihood of bottom snags or rocks catching the weight. This also allows for a more lifelike movement of the fly in the water.

34 HIP BOOT STRAPS

Master fly rod guru Lefty Kreh related a tip long ago about the problems of fishing with hip boots. As manufactured, the adjustable buckle on the outside of the hip boot strap often catches fly lines and ruins the cast. To avoid this, remove the adjustable strap from the buckle, reverse the direction of the strap going through the buckle so that the strap and buckle are on the inside (next to your pant leg) and not able to catch the fly line. It will be a little harder to change the strap adjustment, but does cause fewer tangles when casting.

"The most indispensable item in any fisherman's equipment is his hat. This ancient relic, with its battered crown and well-frayed band, preserves not only the memory of every trout he caught, but also the smell."

—Corey Ford
"Tomorrow's the Day" (1952)

35 SUNSCREEN AND INSECT REPELLENT

Fish can smell sunscreen and insect repellent, so you must keep it off your fishing gear. However, you frequently have to apply and reapply lotions during the day to protect your skin from sunburn and bites. To do this without getting it on your tackle or flies, spread the lotion on the back of one hand and then spread it over your opposite arm, face, ears, back of the neck, front of the neck and anywhere else needed.

Spread some on the back of your other hand to repeat on spots that you cannot reach with your first hand. The result is total protection without ever getting the lotion on the palms of your hands with which you handle tackle and flies.

36 TYING FLIES

One of the best ways to become a better fly fisherman is to tie your own flies. Take a course with a fishing club or local community college, or learn from a friend or basic video on the subject. By learning to tie your own flies, you learn more about the natural insects and foods that flies imitate, how to fish them, how to weight them so that they act naturally, and other features of a good fly. You may not save money, but it is a great winter hobby. In addition, by tying inexpensive flies, you'll more likely fish those flies in impossible places where more big fish lie. Casting a fly you tied for a few cents is not nearly as worrisome as casting a fly you just paid two bucks for two days previously.

37 MAKING WAVES WHEN YOU WADE

Fish react to sound waves. All fish have pores in their scales along a lateral line so that underlying nerve endings can detect water impulses. This means that you must always wade carefully and never create waves that might signal fish that a predator (you!) is in the area. For best results, always wade slowly and carefully.

38 CAMERAS

More and more anglers are releasing fish and using photos to preserve the memories of their days on the water. For this, either film or digital small point-and-shoot cameras are ideal. These small cameras easily fit into a pocket. With one roll of film or one memory card, you can take several dozen pictures to record a day's fishing success and outing.

The best way to protect small point-and-shoot cameras (whether digital or film), is to carry them in a zipper-seal sandwich bag. These bags measure about 7 inches by 8 inches (17.8 cm by 20.3 cm) and are just right for most small cameras. Carry the bagged camera in a top pocket of your fishing vest and only get it out when you are in no danger of falling in or getting wet. Secure the pocket shut so that the camera does not spill out when leaning over to release a fish or check stream-bottom insects. Having a camera at all times makes it easy to get "hero" shots of your buddy with a fish—or for him or her to take shots of you with your catch.

39 PHOTOGRAPHING FISH!

Lots of bass fishermen hold up their catch for a photo by holding the lower jaw of the fish and twisting to force the fish into an angled or horizontal position. This emulates the poses often seen with bass professionals who fish the tournament circuits. But don't do this, particularly if you are into catch-and-release bass fishing! This often strains or breaks the lower jaw of a bass, making it difficult for them to survive when released. Instead, hold or support the rear of the fish as you hold it horizontally, or hold it up straight (vertical) by the lower jaw. If the fish is very large (over 5 pounds/2.3 kg), still support the body of the fish, since this weight hanging from the lower jaw of the fish can injure it.

40 KNEE PADS

The best trout fishermen on small streams wear out the knees of their waders before they wear out the soles. The reason is that anglers kneel to prevent the small stream trout from seeing them, and are thus able to present the fly more carefully and precisely. If you do a lot of this type of fishing, there are ways to prevent wader knee wear. Get comfortable knee pads from a home supply or hardware store. The most comfortable kind fit on with hook-and-loop fastener straps. Keep them in your fishing vest or with your gear to wear when needed.

41 SIMULATING BAITFISH

Pick streamers that simulate local baitfish when choosing streamer flies. Thus, for freshwater trout fishing, pick patterns such as the Black Ghost, Black Nose Dace, White Marabou that simulate dace and small freshwater minnows. For inland striper fishing, pick slab-sided flies that simulate shad that are food for these game fish. For bass and other warm-water fishing, pick fat and dark brown flies such as Muddler Minnows and similar patterns that simulate sculpins and mad toms.

In saltwater, choose large flies such as white and tan Deceivers that simulate mummichogs or killifish, bright-sided patterns that imitate glass minnows or silversides, or very slim, long flies that look like sand lance or eels. Simulating the local baitfish populations is the same as matching the hatch with insects to give the fish what they are used to seeing and eating.

42 FISHING DIFFERENT

It is a mistake to fish the same fly in the same size and color as your fly fishing partner. The reason is that it does not give the fish any choice in "food" selection. By fishing a different fly pattern, size, or color of fly, or fishing at a different depth or with a different retrieve, you give the fish more food options. Once you find that the fish are keying on a certain fly, size, or color, or that fishing a certain way helps, then both of you can capitalize on this knowledge.

43 PRACTICE FLY CASTING REGULARLY

All the best athletes do it—practice, that is. Golfers, gymnasts, and baseball players all practice daily. So should fly anglers. Set up an outfit with a leader and small hank of yarn tied to the leader as a substitute for the fly. Practice all types of casts, including those with high backcasts, wind from various directions, accuracy casts, distance casts, sidearm casts, etc. If possible, practice on water where you can also try the roll cast. If you cast on the lawn, use an old line, since grass is hard on the finish of fly lines. The only cast that you cannot practice on the lawn is a roll cast, basically because there is no water surface tension to hold the line as you make the cast. For this reason, and to get a feel for casting over water, cast on a stream or pond where possible.

44 FALLING IN

No one wants to fall in while fishing. But it can—and does—eventually happen to everyone. What you do next can make the difference in how wet you get. In extreme situations, it can save your life. First, expand your chest or pull on your wader belt immediately to reduce the amount of water getting into your waders. Sometimes you can reduce this to a small trickle. If you can regain your feet, do so immediately. Use your wading staff to help.

If you are in deep water and can't regain your footing, position yourself so that your feet are downstream to fend off any rocks as you float down the river. Hang onto your rod and tackle if possible and try to get to shallow water or a quiet eddy where you can get out. If you take on a lot of water, you might not be able to stand up in shallow water with the weight of water in your waders. In this case, lower your waders and carefully wade to shore. Sit on the bank and raise your legs to pour the water out of each wader leg. Only then stand up, and get back to your camp or vehicle to change clothes.

If you are wet wading (pants, but no waders or hip boots), try to regain your footing, position your feet downstream if floating in deep water, and get out as soon as possible.

In all the above scenarios, a personal floatation device (PFD) such as worn by boaters or a CO_2- or mouth-inflatable yoke air vest is a recommended safety device.

45 HEMOSTATS

Surgeons use hemostats, or clamping forceps; fly anglers also use hemostats. To keep them with you, clamp the jaws onto a pocket flap of your fishing vest, pack, or shirtfront. They are handy for holding small flies when tying knots and especially to remove flies from landed fish. Forceps allow careful clamping and holding of a fly hook so that you can remove the fly from the fish's jaw with minimal damage and handling of the fish. As a result, they are ideal for catch-and-release fishing.

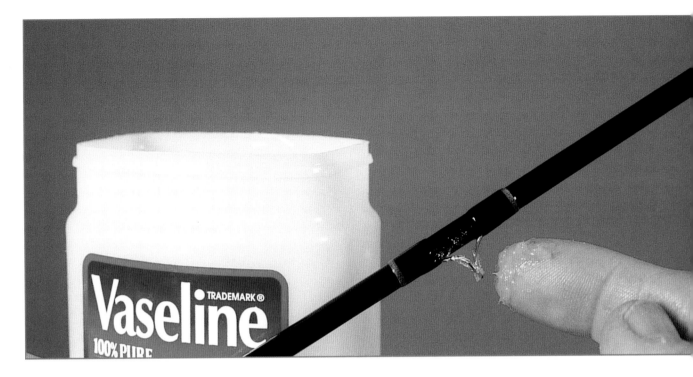

46 ICE IN THE GUIDES

You can do several things when winter fly fishing and ice forms in the guides. The time-honored solution is to dip your rod under the water and swish it around a little to dissolve the ice. This allows making a few more casts until the ice clogs the guides again.

Silicone sprays and homemade anti-freeze sprays help, but you can also get Loon Outdoors Stanley's Ice Off Paste. To use this, which will last longer than any spray, coat the guides with the paste. The paste prevents water from clinging to the guides, thus no ice.

If you can't get Stanley's Ice Off, you can use other products that do about the same thing and won't damage lines. These include standard Vaseline and pure silicone pastes and lubricants, which are available from industrial supply, hardware, and some home products supply companies. All keep water, and thus ice, from forming on the guides. Either wipe these products off or they will wear off in time when you are no longer fishing in freezing temperatures. If you are using petroleum-based products, some of which may affect fly lines, be sure to clean and dress your line after each use.

47 CHEST PACKS

Chest packs are a substitute for fishing vests. They have the advantage of holding the accessories higher on the chest and back. They hold less equipment, but are ideal when you want to wade deep or fish with only a few items, such as in saltwater and tropical fishing. Many sizes and styles are available, some simple fore and aft bags, and others are complex with special tool pockets, and other features.

48 ADDING FLASH

You can add flash easily to any streamer fly while on the water. To do this, carry some of the glitter gel that women use on their bodies for fun and evening wear. Use a small dab rubbed into the wing of any streamer fly to add flash. The gel will wash off as the fly is used, but this also spreads the glitter in the water to simulate scales, thus adding to the attractiveness of the fly. You can also make your own concentrated glitter by mixing fine or coarse glitter from a craft store in a clear gel, such as that used for hair. Store the glitter in a small jar or bottle for instant use in the field. Make sure this is not illegal where you fish.

49 WALKIE-TALKIES

Some of the small and inexpensive walkie-talkies today have a range of up to 5 miles (8 km), and allow easy communication between separated parties. They are ideal for fly anglers fishing different parts of the same stream, or even in different boats. They allow checking on the fishing, trading information on best flies, types of water, retrieve methods, and even water conditions.

You do have to turn them on during the entire time to be able to signal, but there are ways around that also. One method is to keep the radio off to conserve battery power, but to turn it on, "on the hour" to check with one or more buddies. They take little space and work in out-of-the-way areas where the also easy-to-use cell phones do not have service.

"...the things fishermen know about trout aren't facts but articles of faith.

—John Gierach

Trout Bum (1986)

50 BACK BRACES

If you do a lot of wading and are over the age of 25, consider wearing a back brace while wade fishing, suggests expert Chuck Edghill. These large back braces fit tightly around the back and waist. Hook-and-loop fasteners (or suspenders) keep the braces in place. Wear the brace over your shirt, but under your fishing vest. You can loosen the brace when taking a break. The suspenders may help reduce muscle strain when wading for long periods of time and allow you to fish comfortably longer.

51 LIGHTS AT NIGHT

For safety, as well as checking tackle, you need a flashlight for dawn, dusk, and night fishing. For complete safety, carry two flashlights. One should be a regular hand-held flashlight for use at the end of the day to find your way back to the dock if boat fishing, or to pick your way out of the stream if wading. The other should be a minimum-power light for checking tackle and/or tying on flies. For this, the best lights are those with a colored head or filter that casts a blue, green, or red light instead of bright white. There are also specialty lights that can be attached to your hat or cap, worn over your head or cap, pinned to your fishing vest, or stuck in a chest pocket with a gooseneck to angle the light downward. In using any of these lights while fishing, try to minimize casting light on the water, since this might scare fish and affect your fishing success.

52 LIGHT LEVELS

If you have a choice, fish in the very early morning or very late in the day. You can get in some excellent fly fishing in only a few hours by picking the time of day. If you are an early-morning person, plan on getting to the water before dawn, and fish until 10 a.m. or when the fishing slacks off. If you are an evening person, get on the water about four hours before dusk and fish until you can't see your fly or fly line anymore.

53 LIGHTWEIGHT TRAVEL WADERS

Lightweight travel waders are best for all fishing. The other alternative if you fish a lot of different places is to have two pairs of waders—one heavy neoprene for cold weather and a second lightweight pair for warm-weather fishing. Lightweight travel waders are fine for fishing in warm weather, while in cold weather you can insulate them by first donning flannel pajama bottoms or insulated wear under your regular fishing pants.

Chapter 3

Tackle and Tackle Rigging

Making Equipment User Friendly

54 SNELLED HOOK HOLDERS

Fishing large saltwater flies requires a heavy shock, or bite, leader tippet. To keep a fly and short tippet ready rigged, use one of the two types of snelled hook holders used by saltwater surf anglers when bait fishing. One type is a round plastic tube with notches around the opening at one end (for hooks or flies) and a round rubber flange with cuts at the other to hold the mono snell or fly shock leader. You can use these to hold either wire or heavy mono bite leaders.

The other type of snelled hook holder is a flat bracket with openings for the hooks (flies) at one end, and tension spring clips at the other for the snelled leader loop. You can do the same thing with short bite leaders for fly fishing, forming a loop connection in the end of each bite leader. Possibilities for mono include a perfection loop knot, figure-eight knot, or surgeon's loop. For saltwater or warm-water fishing, use the above or a crimped-leader sleeved loop in braided wire or haywire twist in monel wire. These are not leader stretchers, but can hold several or more rigged flies, ready to have the bite leader tied to the tippet.

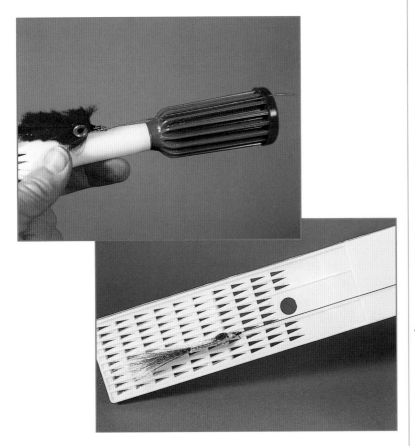

55 GEL SPUN VERSUS DACRON BACKING

Gel spun lines offer a lot of advantages for fly fishermen. The braid is similar to the Dacron used for most backing, is very strong for a given diameter, and has little stretch (less than Dacron). Gel spun lines are being used more often as fly backing.

The disadvantage of the gel spun lines is that most of them are very abrasive and have to be handled carefully. If used wrong, they can cut you; this can be particularly dangerous with line running out of the reel. You cannot hold the line or wrap it around your hand to break off a snag—it will cut. Used carefully, gel spun line can offer more line capacity with greater-strength backing than Dacron.

"Never throw with a long line when a short one will answer your purpose."

—Richard Penn (1833)

Quoted in
The Angler's Weekend Book,

Edited by Eric Taverner
and John Moore

56 SHARPEN HOOKS

The easy way to sharpen hooks is with a diamond hone. For very small flies, run the sides of the hook point on the hone, and then touch it up along the bottom area of the hook point. For larger hooks, run the hone at an angle over the hook point, running the hone side-to-side in the gap of the hook. Then touch it up by running the base of the hook point along the hone to triangulate it.

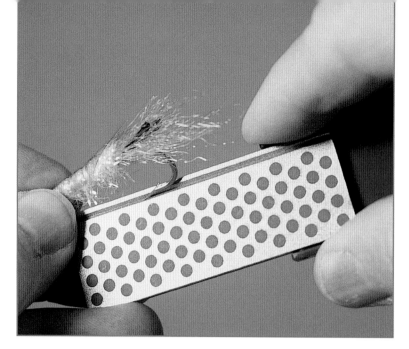

57 MAINTAINING REEL DRAG

Drags work differently in different reels. Some manufacturers seal them and, therefore, the drags do not need lubrication or maintenance. Some drags have special washer materials and require special lubricants or must be used "dry." Many drags have a large cork washer. This creates a braking force when it rubs against the reel spool or a metal plate attached to the spool. You must lubricate these, preferably with neat's-foot oil. You can get kits for this, like the Abel kit containing sealed metal reservoirs of oil, grease, and neat's-foot oil.

58 MIXING GLUES AND SEALERS

I am always looking for a clean place on which to mix two-part glues and cements. One handy solution is to use the top of any canned item. You can turn the can over so that the bottom side is up and use that as your work surface to mix the glue. Expert fly angler Chuck Edghill recommends using a small square of aluminum foil, which he throws away after use.

59 TESTING FLY HOOKS FOR SHARPNESS

Hold the fly in one hand and rest the point on the thumbnail of the opposite hand to test fly hooks for sharpness. Without any pressure, pull the fly across the nail. If the fly hook catches in the nail, the point is sharp. If it slides, the hook needs sharpening. Do not use pressure when doing this—you want to see if the fly hook catches without pressure—not drive the hook through your thumbnail!

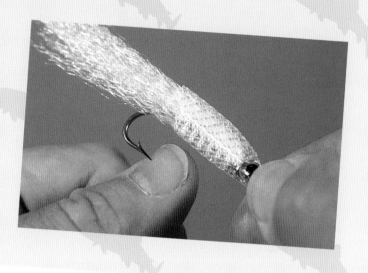

60 FLY HOOK DAMAGE

Check your fly hooks for damage while fishing. This is especially true after snagging something, or if your fly ticks something on the backcast. Flies break when they hit rocks. Check for dull flies by touching the point to your thumbnail and sharpening if necessary.

61 SHARPENING HOOKS

Diamond dust fingernail files, available in every drugstore, are ideal for sharpening fly hooks. They are very thin, so that they can work easily in the gap of small flies to triangulate hooks. They are also inexpensive and easy to replace. Buy several, and keep one in each fishing vest, fanny pack, shoulder pack, leader wallet, or wader pouch.

"How can you possibly say you just had a wonderful day? It has been windy, cold, spitting snow and all you caught were a couple of 10-inch trout." My question was from the wife of a non-fishing friend. I tried to respond intelligently about my love of the sport. The beautiful places we fish, the wildlife we often see, the fun of just casting ...Later, I revisited the conversation and again struggled with a simple answer to her question.

Just what is the attraction? I think maybe it is that last multiple-choice test answer, "All of the Above." So, next time a non-fishing friend asks, I'll just change the subject."

—Pete Van Gytenbeek
CEO/President, Federation of Fly Fishers

62 LANYARDS AND RETRACTABLE REELS

To prevent losing gear, use lanyards or retractable pull cords that are stored in small reels. Often these are generically called "zingers." Lanyards are good for fishing pliers, wading staffs, clippers, nippers, dry fly dressing bottles, nets, and similar gear. Small ones for nippers and clippers are available from all fly shops. Larger, heavy-duty models are necessary for holding pliers, landing nets, wading staffs, etc. The best of these currently available are the Hammerhead Gear Keepers, which come in many styles, different attachment methods, and also different strengths and pull tensions.

63 BACKING SIZE

Generally, anglers consider 20-pound (9.1-kg) Dacron backing the standard for most fly fishing. Those after big fish (sharks, large tarpon, billfish, or large snook) or when fishing in snaggy areas, choose 30-pound (13.6-kg) Dacron. Some fly anglers after tuna use 50-pound (22.7-kg) Dacron backing because of the possibility of the tail of a tuna hitting, abrading, and breaking lighter backing. If after fish no larger than 20 pounds (9.1 kg) under normal fishing conditions, choose 20-pound-test (9.1-kg) backing. If after larger fish, choose 30-pound (13.6-kg) Dacron backing. As listed above, gel spun lines also offer an alternative that provides you with stronger backing and increased line capacity.

64 CASES FOR SPLIT SHOT

If you are fishing with only one size of split shot, an easy container is an empty Tic Tac box or similar flip-top candy container. These have snap caps and make it easy to dispense one, or a few, split shot at a time. Never leave these containers where they could be confused for treats, and never use these containers for food products again. Mark the size of split shot in each container with a black felt-tip marker.

TACKLE AND TACKLE RIGGING

65 A SIMPLE LANYARD

You can make a simple lanyard for pliers by using one of the plastic coil-spring key chains available for a few bucks at most discount stores. To do this, use the split ring end to attach to the pliers, and attach a clip or snap on the other end to your fishing vest or wader belt. You can use these, which stretch several feet, without risking loss. They also work with nets and other gear.

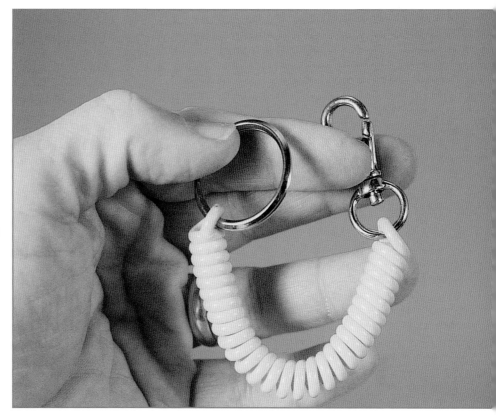

66 UP-LOCKING/ DOWN-LOCKING REEL SEATS

Fly rod reel seats have knurled locking collets to secure the sliding hood onto the foot of the reel. These are available as up-locking (with the sliding hood and collet nut at the bottom) or down-locking (with the collet nut and threads at the top). The best for most fishing is the up-locking style, since this provides for a slight "extension butt." This protects the reel from damage when resting the rod on the ground, or allows you to rest the rod against your body to better fight big fish without the reel tangling in your clothing.

67 EXTRA SPOOLS

Lots of fly reels today are expensive, but a simple way around both the cost and multi-line problem is to buy spare spools for different fishing situations. Spools are less expensive than a new reel and most reels allow easy spool exchange with a flip lever on the front of the spool. Thus, you can change to the line of choice before each trip, or carry a spare spool in your vest to switch from floating to sinking-tip to sinking lines or shooting heads. Just make sure that the spools that you buy are an exact fit for the reel, and that the spool holds both the line and necessary backing for the fishing you plan to do.

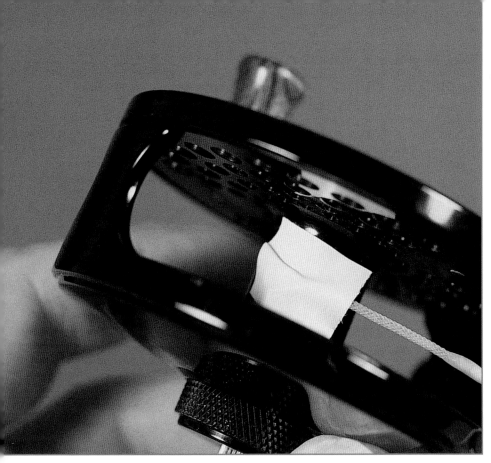

68 PREVENTING LINE SLIP

With today's highly polished reels, the backing arbor knot can slip on the reel if a fish takes enough line to run the end of the backing close to the reel spool arbor. If this happens, the line may slip, making it impossible to retrieve line. To prevent this, run the backing line around the spool arbor twice and then make a slipknot around the standing line with the tag end. Pull tight. Finally, add a small piece of masking tape over the line connection and arbor knot to prevent slippage. The subsequent line wrapped over this piece of tape prevents the tape from coming off or the line from slipping.

69 EXTENSION BUTTS

In the past, many fly rods for large fish had long extension butts of up to 6 inches (15.2 cm) in length. These caused more problems than they cured. While they did allow some separation of the fly reel from the angler's body, they also often caught loops of fly line on the cast, causing break-offs. To prevent this, use an up-locking reel seat with a very short extension butt of no more than 2 inches (5 cm). You still get enough separation of the fly outfit from your body and clothing, but will reduce the risk of catching the fly line.

70 ALTERNATIVES TO LEAD

Many anglers worry about using lead fishing products. Also, more and more states, Canadian provinces, and regulated areas are banning lead used in fishing equipment. The reason is that lead is toxic to all living things. Most lead in fly fishing tackle is in lead-core lines used for making sinking shooting heads, in split shot and other sinker choices, in lead wire wrapped onto a hook for weight when tying a fly, and lead dumbbell eyes used for the same purpose. This ban also often includes brass products, since lead is a component of brass.

Substitutes include products of tungsten, bismuth, and tin. Check your local regulations about use of lead, and contact your local fly shop for lead substitutes.

71 WADING STAFFS

Some anglers make a point of visiting flea markets and garage sales to buy ski poles for their buddies and fishing clubs. Often they can get ski poles for less than a dollar. These make great, although slightly short, wading staffs for fly fishing. You can use them in one of two ways. One way is to keep the ski pole as it is for wading on sandy or mucky bottoms, since the webbing (usually plastic these days) at the bottom serves as a "snowshoe" to prevent the pole from sinking deep.

The second way is to carefully remove (try wire cutters or a hacksaw) the plastic webbing to make a straight pole for rocky streams. Add a lanyard that you can attach to your bootstrap or fishing vest to prevent loss of the recycled wading staff.

72 CHANGING DRAG

The best drag setting on a reel is a light drag. Too heavy a drag will break off a fish, since the water resistance of line is often enough drag to keep a fish from coming unbuttoned. One way to check a drag directly off of the reel is to hold the leader in your mouth and pull out line with your lips until you can no longer pull line. This will usually be a drag of 1 or 2 pounds (0.5 or 0.9 kg).

There are several ways to increase drag. One is to palm the reel on those reels (most of them) that have an external palming rim. The next best way is to raise the rod to about a 45-degree angle. This increases the functional drag (not the drag off of the reel) through the friction of the line going through the guides. Note that water resistance on the thick line also creates drag on any run.

Use all three of these methods. An added advantage of raising the rod to 45 degrees is that the limber rod provides insurance against the leader tippet breaking.

73 ROD BAGS

Many fly rod bags from manufacturers have a tie cord at the top; some also have a tie cord in the middle. If you use these, make sure that you tie loosely to prevent the rod from bending or warping during storage when in the rod tube. Use a very loose bowknot in these situations or just wrap the ends of the cord around the top of the bag after folding over the end flap.

74 TURLE KNOT

The Turle knot is an old knot, but still a good one for tying your leader tippet to your fly. Anglers most often use Turle knots with dry flies, but you should only use it with flies tied on hooks with turned-up or turned-down eyes. This is because the leader goes through the eye of the hook with the knot tied around the hook shank/head of the fly in back of the eye. Thus, tying this on a straight eye hook results in the leader tippet adversely kinked up or down.

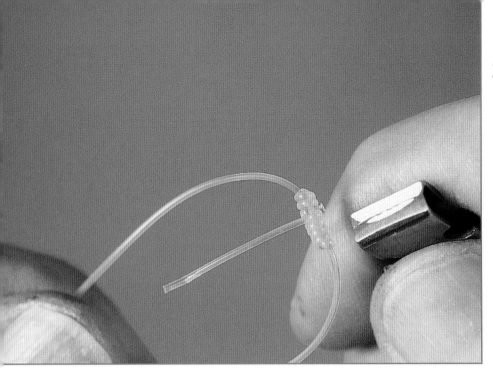

75 TRIMMING KNOTS

When tying knots and pulling them up securely, make sure that you trim the knot properly. To do this, use nippers or nail clippers to cut the tag end of the line close to the knot. The cutters on most pliers are seldom good for this, since they often do not allow close cutting. If you leave an extended tag end, the knot is no stronger, and you'll catch more algae or cause a sinking leader to float longer. Remember, tighten securely, and then trim closely.

77 CUTTING KNOTS

"Wind knots" are overhand knots that occur in fly leaders while casting. While we call them wind knots, really they are the result of poor casting (perhaps a gust of wind now and again) that causes the leader to wrap and knot around itself. If the wind knot is loose, it is easy to untie it, straighten the leader, and keep on fishing. If the knot is tight, break or cut it and retie the leader, using a five-turn blood knot. Trim the knot ends closely. A tip from Chuck Edghill is to use two hook points (two flies) to pull apart a loosened knot.

76 FLOATING LINES

To get just under the surface, fish a sinking or lightly weighted fly with a floating line. The floating line will suspend the fly while the lightly weighted fly will sink and fish the upper part of the water column. For this, you can use any floating line and should use a long leader of 7 1/2 to 9 feet (2.3 m to 2.7 m) or longer. The length and retrieve speed along with the weight of the fly controls the depth of the fly fished.

When picking a fly, make sure that you choose one with only a little weight so that it does not cause the floating line to sink unnecessarily. Best flies are those with only a few wraps of lead on the forward part of the hook shank, or with a metal bead or dumbbell eyes for a little weight. Front weighting the fly helps to give it more movement when you work in a twitching retrieve.

"We have been oversold on the short rod."

—Vincent C. Marinaro

In the Ring of the Rise
(1976)

78 LUBRICATING KNOTS

When you pull a knot tight in monofilament, it creates friction. Friction creates heat, which can be damaging to line and knot strength. To prevent this, and to ensure tight and secure knots, lubricate the loose knot with saliva, and then pull the knot tight. This both lubricates the knot to prevent friction and heat and also allows you to pull the knot very tight. Also, experts say saliva masks odors that might scare fish.

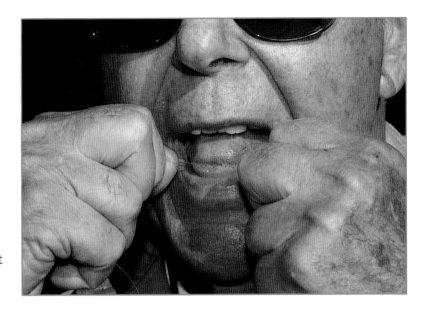

79 STRIKE INDICATORS

An alternative way to fish deep is to use a sinking line and a floating strike indicator on the leader. To do this, fish a full-sinking line to get and keep the fly deep. You can use any length leader for this method, including long leaders that you would normally use for floating lines. Tie on the fly of your choice. (It does not have to be a floating fly, as with sinking lines.) Then place a strike indicator about 18 to 24 inches (45.7 to 61.0 cm) up from the fly to help float the fly and keep it from snagging on the bottom.

For this, use a foam or buoyant strike indicator, not the popular yarn that would absorb water and not provide flotation. The result is that you can fish any fly in any situation as deep as you can get a fly line without the risk of getting hung up. This is an ideal way to fish streamer flies deep to imitate baitfish.

80 MARKING ROD SECTIONS

Many rod manufacturers make similar-size fly rods on the same blank and then through an external grinding process adjust the blank weight and action to the desired line weight. This makes it almost impossible to ever get the right rod sections back together if you mix up several three- or four-piece travel rods of the same brand. To prevent mix-up of rod sections, mark each section with a dot of colored paint that can help to line up the guides as well as identify the rod sections.

Use different color dots for different rods and double dots if you have a lot of rods and run out of colors. For best results, use a waterproof enamel, lacquer, or acrylic-based paint. To mark the rod, touch a pin or finishing nail head to the paint, and then touch it to the rod at the ferrule location and in line with the rod guides.

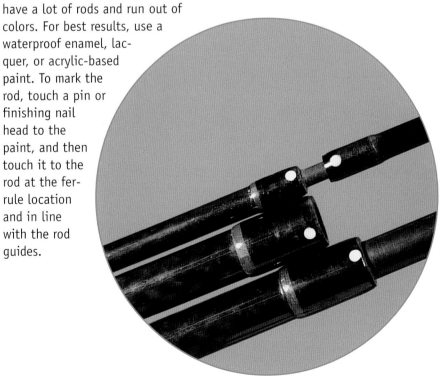

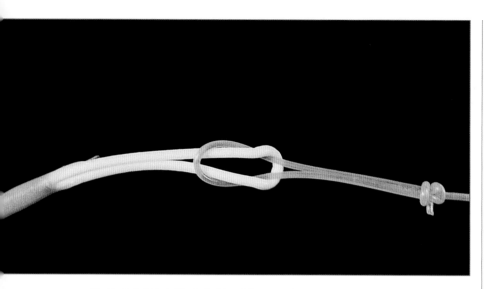

82 LOOP-TO-LOOP CONNECTIONS

Nail knots used to be very popular for line and leader or backing connections. Today, consider the advantages of the loop-to-loop connection. If you have a spliced or knotted loop in your backing, a loop in each end of your fly line, and a loop in your leader butt, you can easily change anything, anytime you wish. This allows you to change lines from a floating to sinking or sinking-tip while fishing, to change complete leaders, or to add some mini lead heads between the line and the leader to help sink the fly.

There are many ways to do this, including braided loop sleeves, tied-on mono loops, etc., but the best way to add a loop in your fly line is to fold over and wrap the end of the line itself. This eliminates other weak links in the chain. To do this, fold over the end of the fly line, hold the folded end part with some fly-tying thread on a bobbin, and twirl the bobbin around the folded line while holding the loop end with the other hand. After wrapping the loop with fly-tying thread, make a whip finish in the line to complete it. Clip the excess thread and then seal the wrap with flexible glue, such as Ultra Flex.

83 SPOOLING LINE

You don't want to underfill or overfill your fly reel. But it is difficult to tell how much backing any reel takes if you put the backing on first. To fill a reel properly, first spool on the fly line, front end first, then connect and tie on the backing, and continue to fill the reel with the backing until within about 1/8 inch (3.175 mm) of the spool capacity. Reverse all of this onto another reel of equal or larger capacity. This does not have to be a fly reel; it can be any large spool to hold the line temporarily. Then spool the line again onto another large reel, and finally back onto the original reel. This switching of the line will put the backing on first, followed by the fly line, all with the right amount of line to properly fill your reel.

81 MORE BACKING CAPACITY

Need more backing on your fly reel? You can get some by cutting back the rear portion of any weight-forward line that you are using and using the added space for backing. This is easy to do the next time you change lines or do reel maintenance. Note you can only do this with level or weight-forward lines—you do not want to cut back a double-taper line. Cutting back the fly line usually makes little practical difference to your fishing, while adding backing insurance. Most lines are about 90 to 105 feet (27.4 to 32.0 m) long.

If you don't cast the entire line, it becomes unnecessary bulk on the reel. For example, if your maximum casting range is about 60 feet (18 m), cut back the line to 70 feet (21.3 m) [keep 10 feet (3.0 m) of line for insurance] and use the rest of the reel capacity for backing. Note that you must cut the line from the rear—the running portion only! Then follow the tips for adding any fly line and backing (see Adding Backing to the Reel on page 46) to fill the reel properly and completely.

84 ATTACHING NETS TO VESTS

Attach a landing net to the D-ring located on the back of all fishing vests. This is the best way to carry a landing net while stream fishing. (If your vest does not have a D-ring, you can add a key-style split ring to the strap or use a short cloth strap to sew a D-ring in place.) Buy a French snap from a hardware store and attach it to the end of the landing net. These snaps are unlike dog leash snaps in that you operate them by squeezing the two arms or sides to open the snap in the middle. This makes it easy to remove the net hung from your back by reaching around to unsnap it. Carrying the net on the back center of your vest also reduces the possibility of the net catching on tree limbs and brush.

85 SEALING FLY LINE LOOPS

Seal fly line loops to protect them by using flexible glue, such as Pliobond, Ultra Flex, or similar flexible cement. If the glue is too thick, consider diluting it with a solvent. Check the label for the correct thinning solvent or call the manufacturer (most manufacturers list a toll-free number on the glue container that you can call for information). Once the glue is diluted to the proper consistency, apply it to the wrapped section of the fly line only, using a bodkin or small disposable brush. If you are using the popular Ultra Flex to seal your fly line loops, you can use acetone fingernail polish remover for dilution. It is similar to MEK (methyl ethyl ketone), the basic solvent for this glue.

86 VEST LENGTH

If you wear chest-high waders and often fish deep, get a "shorty" fishing vest to prevent the vest from getting wet. If you are fishing in hip boots, a full-length vest gives you more room and pockets. An alternative to the shorty vest for deep-wading fly anglers is to wear a long vest, but wear it inside your waders if there is enough room.

87 MAKING ROD BAGS

You can buy fly rod bags or you can make your own. Why buy or make a fly rod bag when the rod came in a rod case? The reason is that more and more rods are coming in cases that have attached partition bags—i.e., they are part of the case and do not come out, as did the separate bags in aluminum cases of the past. I make rod bags from remnants of flannel cloth sold inexpensively at fabric stores.

Be sure to buy enough material to make the style and number of bags that you want. If you are working with three- or four-piece rods, you can get by with 1 yard (0.9 m) to make several bags. If you have two-piece 9- to 10-foot (2.7- to 3.0-meter) rods [half the rod measures 4½ to 5 feet (1.4 to 1.5 m)], you will need 2 yards (1.8 m) of material, unless the material is wide enough. Fifty-four inches (137.2 cm) is about the maximum width of most materials; and some are only 36 inches (91.4 cm) wide.

To make a bag, fold over a piece of cloth to make the bag the right length and diameter for your rods. For four-piece rods, 9 feet (2.7 m) long, make the bag about 10 inches by 32 inches (25.4 cm by 81.3 cm). For two-piece, 9-feet-long (2.7-m) rods, make bags 5 inches (12.7 cm) wide by 59 to 60 inches (149.9 to 152.4 cm) long. The extra length in each of these allows the top flap to fold over. The width varies on these cases, since travel rods require four slots; two-piece rods require only two slots. Make the bags wider on rods that have extra-large grips, extension butts, or large stripping guides.

88 LABELING ROD BAGS

Mark all rod bags, commercial or homemade, with pertinent information. You might choose to mark the line weight, rod length, brand, or something else. Mark the bag at the top flap with a permanent felt-tip marker. With black or very dark bags, sew on a strip of white cloth and mark the cloth with the information. This helps when getting ready for any trip to prevent taking the wrong rod and not realizing it until too late. You don't want to pull out your 3-weight when getting to Alaska expecting to find a 10-weight for big king salmon.

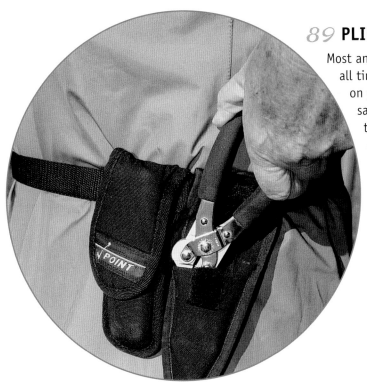

89 PLIERS

Most anglers carry sheathed fishing pliers at all times. The easy way to carry pliers is on your wader safety belt. If fishing in saltwater, nylon sheaths are better than leather sheaths. Wash out nylon sheaths as required. Leather sheaths soak up and hold salt, which can be detrimental to any equipment.

90 MARK LINE FOR PICK-UP

Years ago, Scientific Anglers introduced a line that had a slightly swollen area for several inches at the point where you should pick up the line for the next backcast. The purpose was to give fly anglers a tactile signal where to pick up a given fly line off the water for the next cast. While it was designed with the beginner or inexperienced fly angler in mind, it was handy for any angler. This great idea remains in the Scientific Anglers' beginners Headstart lines with the Telecast bump, but you can do the same thing on any fly line using one of two methods.

One method is to mark the fly line for an inch or two (2.5 to 5 cm) along this "sweet spot," using a permanent felt-tip marker. While it is not tactile, you can see this marked part of the line coming into the guides to signal when to pick up for the next cast. The other method is to tie a long nail knot around the line at this spot using 10- to 20-pound-test (4.5- to 9.1-kg) mono. Clip the tag ends short. You can feel this pick-up point as the line runs through your hands. To determine this spot, rig your rod complete with a practice fly (no hook) and practice over water to find the best spot to pick up the line considering your fishing and casting ability. Then mark the line at this point.

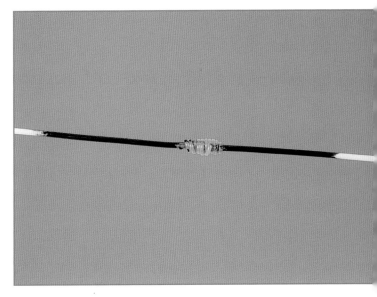

Do this with each outfit, since it varies with the weight and type of line used. You can also combine these methods, marking the line for a visual signal as well as wrapping it with mono for a tactile signal, or combine both with a wrap of bright fluorescent mono. You can do this only on floating or sinking-tip lines, since sinking lines must be retrieved most of the way in and pulled out of the water to make an aerial roll cast.

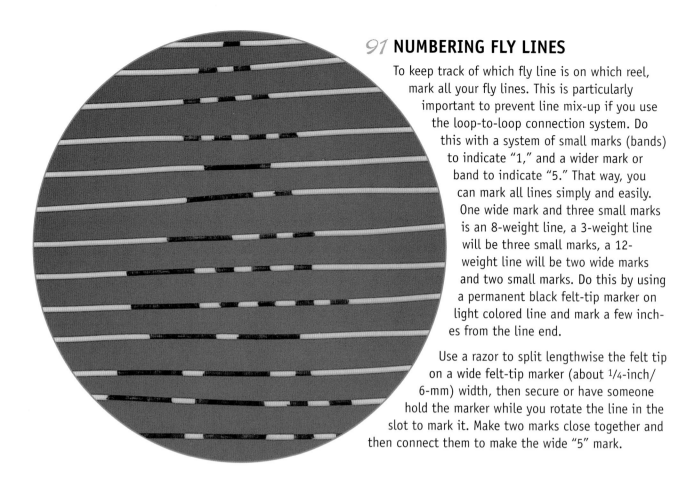

91 NUMBERING FLY LINES

To keep track of which fly line is on which reel, mark all your fly lines. This is particularly important to prevent line mix-up if you use the loop-to-loop connection system. Do this with a system of small marks (bands) to indicate "1," and a wider mark or band to indicate "5." That way, you can mark all lines simply and easily. One wide mark and three small marks is an 8-weight line, a 3-weight line will be three small marks, a 12-weight line will be two wide marks and two small marks. Do this by using a permanent black felt-tip marker on light colored line and mark a few inches from the line end.

Use a razor to split lengthwise the felt tip on a wide felt-tip marker (about 1/4-inch/ 6-mm) width, then secure or have someone hold the marker while you rotate the line in the slot to mark it. Make two marks close together and then connect them to make the wide "5" mark.

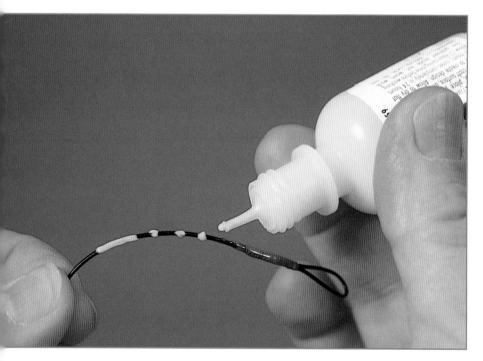

92 MARKING SINKING LINE SINK RATES

To mark the line weight of sinking or sinking-tip lines (which are usually black or very dark) or any dark line, use bright or white fabric paint. This thick paint is water-based acrylic, but becomes waterproof when cured for 24 hours. Mark the lines the same way you would mark floating lines with the wide and narrow bands for "5" and "1" respectively. The marking diminishes in time, but is easy to restore using the same steps above.

93 RATTLE FLIES

Fly anglers argue over rattles in flies. Many anglers swear by them, especially when fishing for species such as pike, redfish, stripers, and largemouth bass. They can attract fish, since bait makes noise that attracts game fish. Crayfish, for example, make clicking noises with their claws as they move or when they feel stressed or threatened. In all cases, rattles may not help, but they certainly do not hurt.

Situations where rattle flies shine include fishing deep and fishing in muddy, or murky, water. Often these flies are at their best when visibility is limited. The best way to fish these flies is with a series of slight twitches to cause the rattles to make continuous noise. The best flies are head-weighted so that each twitch throws the rattle to the back of the chamber to make noise and each pause causes the rattle to slide forward as the head of the fly sinks first.

94 MARKING FLY LINES

All line companies (the industry is slowly working on this) may ultimately standardize sink rates on lines. The standards as proposed use a number that approximates the sink rate in inches per second. Thus, a 2-sink-rate line sinks at about 1½ to 2½ inches (3.8 to 6.4 cm) per second; a 5-sink-rate sinks at a rate of about 4½ to 5½ inches (11 to 14 cm) per second. This eliminates the confusion of terms, such as "intermediate," "slow sinking," "fast sinking," etc.

Mark the sink rate of your lines by using the same numbering system used for marking the line weight, but mark the line about 12 to 18 inches (30.5 to 45.7 cm) above the end where the line weight is marked. Most sinking or sinking-tip lines are dark and require the light-colored fabric paint, but you can mark light-colored lines with a felt-tip marker.

95 MORE ON MARKING FLY LINES

Another way to mark fly lines is to use your computer. This tip, from Softex creator John Ryzanych of Icon, involves typing out the necessary information on your computer and printing it on standard paper. Once you do this, cut out the information and roll each small slip of paper around a small round rod, such as a straightened paper clip or bodkin. Then, with the paper curled into a tight roll, use Softex to glue the paper information onto the fly line a few inches above the end. You may wish to wrap fly-tying thread or some light mono around the paper to make sure that it stays in a tight wrap around the fly line.

Once the Softex cures, coat the paper with Softex to protect it. This allows inclusion of more information than the "band" marking system, since you can type in data, such as line weight, sink rate, tropical or cold weather, brand, style or model, length, etc. Use a very small font size to fit on the line.

> *"Just as in cooking there's no such thing as a little garlic, in fishing there's no such thing as a little drag."*
>
> —H. G. Tapply
>
> *The Sportsman's Notebook* (1964)

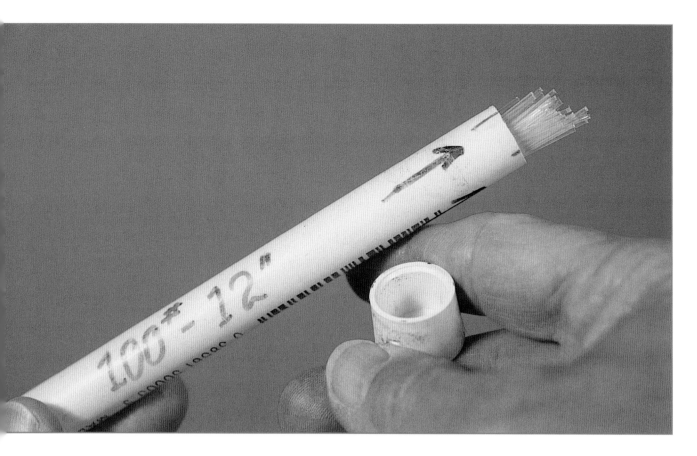

96 STORING LEADERS

To store mono in 50- to 200-pound-test (22.7- to 90.7-kg) lengths for shock tippets, make a leader section case. For this, get a length of 1/2-inch (13-mm) PVC pipe, glue and cap one end, and buy a second slip-on friction cap for the other end. Make the case about 1/2 inch longer than the lengths of mono stored. Use a permanent felt-tip marker to mark the pound-test measurement of the mono stored inside and the length of the leader material. Mark the slip-on cap end so you know which end to remove.

97 PREPARING LEADERS

For some fishing (tarpon and big snook), you will need a heavy shock or bite leader between the fly and the tippet. Something from about 50- to 200-pound-test (22.7- to 90.7-kg) is standard. The problem is that when fishing, it is almost impossible to stretch this heavy leader material to make it straight. One solution is to cut a board the length you want the leader sections, and notch it at both ends. Wrap the chosen mono tightly around the board lengthwise. Then "cook" the mono for a few minutes in a pot of boiling water.

If you do not have a big enough pot, make a dipping tank from a length of 2-inch (5-cm) PVC pipe, glued and capped at one end. Secure this upright, add the mono-wrapped board, and pour in the boiling water. (If holding the PVC, use a funnel to pour the water and hold it with a potholder to prevent burns.) Allow the mono to sit in the boiling water for a few minutes, then remove the mono board and immediately place it in ice-cold water.

The boiling water "relaxes" the mono into a stretched, straight length, while the cold water "sets" it in this state. Once the mono is set, remove it from the cold water, cut off the ends where it went around the board, and save it in straight lengths to use as a shock tippet.

98 ROD TUBES

Aluminum rod tubes are great for protecting your rods, but the caps are easily lost. To prevent this, tie the cap to the top of the rod tube. There are two ways to do this. One is to use heavy mono, nylon cord, or scrap fly line to tie securely around the top of the rod tube, then extend the end of the cord through the hole in the middle of the cap and tie a knot to prevent the cord from pulling through the hole. If the hole is too large for a knot, add a small bead or button to the cord before making the knot.

You can also drill a small hole in the top side of the rod tube (remove the rod first, for obvious reasons!). Drill a hole in the center of the cap (if it lacks one) and then thread cord through the two holes, knotting as above to keep the cap in place and attached to the tube.

99 BREAKING TIPPET

If you hook a snag or tree with your fly and the fly wraps around the branches or tangles in the leaves, it is easier to snap the fly tippet, remove the fly, and pull the leader free. This is easier than holding the snag or tree while trying to thread the fly through the tangle. Once you have the fly and the rest of the tippet free, then you can check the leader for abrasion, make any necessary replacements, and retie the fly for fishing.

Another tip is to break off the twig or branch and then at your leisure, unwrap the leader and tippet from the foliage. This is also best to do if you are working from a boat that can drift around, making it difficult to hold position and get the fly free.

100 HOOK GAP

Most flies have a good hook gap—the distance between the shank and the point at which a fish is well hooked. Carefully check flies with full bodies or those with deer-hair-spun bodies, such as many bass bugs. These flies, if the deer hair is incorrectly trimmed, may have enough of a hair body to block part of the gap and prevent good hooking. To correct flies that have a blocked gap, use trimming scissors to cut away materials in the gap area. Make sure you do not cut the fly-tying thread as you do this.

101 ADDING BACKING TO THE REEL

To add backing correctly to the reel, first tie an arbor knot, then place a piece of tape over the loop knot to secure the line to the arbor. Next, secure the reel on a rod and crank the line onto the reel, running the line through a heavy work glove or clean rag. Note that fly reels do not have a level wind as do bait-casting reels, nor the reciprocating shaft of spinning reels, both designed to place the line evenly on the spool.

Use the little finger of your glove/rag hand to control the line and guide it side-to-side on the reel for neat, even spooling. By spooling the line tight on the reel, you reduce the chance that the line will dig into previously spooled layers of line when a fish makes a run, causing a break-off as the line pinches. This system is best for all backing lines (preferably Dacron) and very important if you are using the newer gel-spun lines for backing.

An alternative to this method is to spool the line on extra tightly, using one of the newer line spooling machines designed for all reels and spools, such as the Cyclone Line Winder from Pure Fishing.

"To the fisherman born there is nothing so provoking of curiosity as a fishing rod in a case."

—Roland Pertwee
"The River God" (1928)

102 LEADER FORMULA 50/30/20

One simple formula for fly leaders is the 50/30/20 formula, which makes the butt section of the leader 50 percent of the leader length, the tapered portion 30 percent of the length, and the tippet 20 percent of the total length. This means that with a heavy, 10-foot-long (3.0-meter) saltwater leader with a 12-pound-test (5.4-kg) tippet, you would use 5 feet (1.5 m) of 40- to 50-pound-test (18.1- to 22.7-kg) butt section, 3 feet (0.9 m) of tapered section of from about 30- to 15-pound-test (13.6- to 6.8-kg) [three sections of 1 foot (0.3 m) each of 30-, 20-, and 15-pound-test (13.6-, 9.1-, and 6.8-kg)] and 2 feet (0.6 m) of 12-pound-test (5.4-kg) tippet.

Use blood knots for all of these leader section connections. If using a loop-to-loop connection with the line, tie a surgeon's, figure-eight, or perfection loop knot. All ensure that the loop stays aligned with the leader.

Other factors can be colors of monos, which (when mixed) might alert fish to something unnatural tied to your fly. In standard leader kits, all the monos included are the same brand and type. If you do use different brands of mono, use the stiffer one for the butt section and the limp one for the tippet.

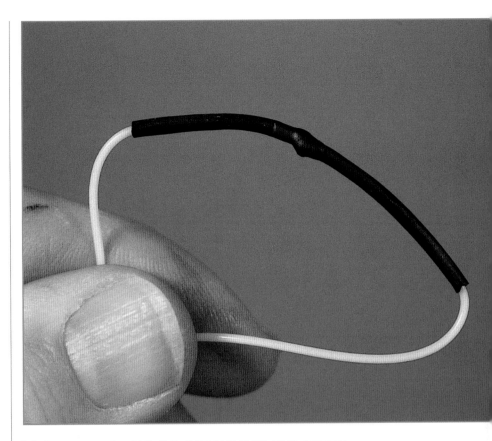

103 CONNECTING OR REPAIRING FLY LINES

Once, while walking a rocky bank, I stepped on a dragging fly line and completely severed it on a sharp rock. If this ever happens, or if you damage a short section of line, you can repair it. To do this, buy a splicing kit, such as those available from Gudebrod. The freshwater kit includes spools of 25- and 35-pound-test (11.3- and 15.9-kg) braided mono, while the saltwater kit has 35- and 50-pound-test (15.9- and 22.7-kg) braided mono.

To use these or similar kits, insert the cut fly line into the two ends of a 3-inch (7.6-cm) length of the smallest size possible of braided mono sleeve. Then, make a nail knot around each end of the mono braid sleeve, or use your fly-tying thread to tightly wrap the two ends and complete with a whip finish. Seal with flexible cement or glue (use the glue provided or use Softex or Ultra Flex). When you do this, make sure that you butt the ends of the fly line in the sleeve to prevent any hinging effect on the finished repair.

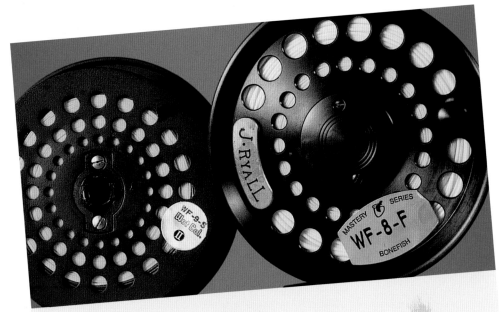

104 MARKING FLY SPOOLS

Mark your fly reels with the line size and any other particulars of the line (tropical or cold weather, sink rate, etc.). Do this on the side plate of the reel with a small self-stick label or with a label maker. Protect the label with a covering of clear tape. You also can do this on the outside or the inside of the reel spool. If placing the label on the inside of a spool, make sure that it doesn't interfere with any of the pawls, gearing, or drag mechanisms of the reel as the spool turns. Many manufacturers sell fly lines with self-stick markers for this purpose.

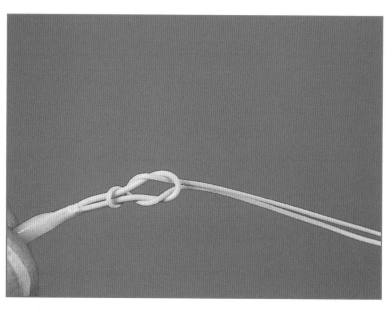

105 DOUBLE LOOP OF BACKING

The thicker and stiffer fly line loop can sometimes cause a loop-to-loop connection of Dacron backing and fly line to slip into an ineffective girth hitch, where the Dacron backing loops around itself. To prevent this, run the reel twice through the large backing loop so that there is an extra turn of backing around the fly line to keep the loop-to-loop connection secure.

106 SECURING LOOSE REELS

Sometimes, reels will be slightly loose on a reel seat. This can be as a result of the reel seat having too long a barrel for the short reel foot, having thin reel foot ends that are loose under the hoods, or reel feet not wide enough to fill the reel seat hoods. To prevent the resulting reel seat wobble, wrap a rubber band around the non-threaded part of the reel seat barrel. Make sure that you have several turns of the rubber band and that they do not overlap each other. Then, when you slide the reel foot into the fixed hood, the rubber band will create extra pressure and space on the reel seat/reel foot area to keep the reel from sliding around.

If you wish a permanent solution, get a wide rubber band and glue one or more sections of it to just the reel seat area where the reel foot touches the reel seat.

107 SINKING SHOOTING HEADS

Most shooting lines are sinking style. You can also make your own from lead or lead-free trolling line. Realize that the strength of a lead-core trolling line is in the braided sleeve. To get maximum sink rate of the line, use as light a line as possible, since most lines use the same-diameter lead or non-lead product, and the thinner diameter of the light line creates less water resistance and sinks faster.

To make the line attachment to the running line, fold over the end, wrap it tightly with fly-tying thread, add a whip finish, and seal it with Pliobond or Ultra Flex. Make a similar loop in the front end for attaching a short leader with a loop-to-loop connection. Splice, or tie, a similar larger loop on the end of the braided running line, or make a wrapped, whip-finished loop if using level fly line for the running line. Make a similar loop in the other end of the running line for loop-to-loop attachment to the fly line backing. Spool all the parts on the reel—backing, 100 feet (30.5 m) of running line, and 30 feet (9.1 m) of shooting head—and you are ready to fish.

108 SLIP STRIKE WITH LIGHT TIPPETS

Striking a fish when using a very light tippet may break the tippet if you are not careful. To guard against this, use a "slip strike." For this, don't hold on to the line when you strike. Instead, allow the line to slip through your fingers and rod guides as you make a striking twitch with the rod. This exerts enough pressure on the hook to bury it in the fish, while allowing the line to slip so that you do not overtax the leader and break the tippet. It is a simple technique that takes some time to get used to by allowing the line to slip or slide as you twitch the rod on a strike. Practice this, since it seems foreign to our natural tendency to set the hook with a hard strike.

109 MINI LEAD HEADS

If you don't want to buy a sinking or sinking-tip fly line but still want to fish deep, there is an easy solution. Use "mini lead heads," as I call them, which are nothing more than short lengths of lead-core (or non-lead-core) line with a loop in each end to attach into your loop-to-loop system between the line and the leader or in the middle of the leader. If you do attach these in the middle of the leader, you must use loops between your butt leader section and the tapered leader portion. You can buy these mini lead heads (Orvis, Cortland, and Gudebrod, among others, make them) or you can make them using lead-core trolling line. You can also use lead-free trolling line, which is available from several manufacturers, including Gudebrod. The commercial mini lead heads are 2- to 6-feet (0.6- to 1.8-m) long, and have neat braided loops on each end. To make your own, use 27- to 30-pound-test (12.2- to 13.6-kg) lead-core line. Cut the mini head to the length that you want. I like 2-foot-long (0.6-m) lengths, which can be used individually or looped together to make longer lengths for deeper fishing or heavier outfits.

Fold over the ends to make a loop and whip-finish it with fly-tying thread (see Loop-To-Loop Connections on page 38 for details), or make a simple Homer Rhode knot in the end. In either case, seal the knot or the loop wrap with a flexible glue or cement. (See Sealing Fly Line Loops on page 39 for details.)

110 CAMOUFLAGE YOUR LINES

It goes without saying that trout spook easily. They even spook with the solid color of fly line in the water. To camouflage your line, strip it from the reel, wrap it around your hand or a large box (a cereal box is ideal), and then randomly mark the line with different-color, permanent felt-tip markers. Good colors are black, green, brown, blue, gray, and tan. Neatness does not count here, since any random coloring keeps the line from looking like a straight stick of color and thus makes it less visible to fish.

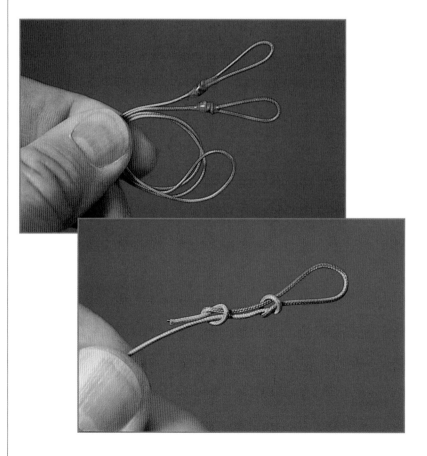

111 SECURING A SLIDING HOOD

Reels that have a single collet nut and a sliding hood can become loose while fishing. To prevent this, get an O-ring from your hardware store that will stretch over the rod butt and is no larger than the diameter of the collet nut. Slide this in place between the collet nut and the sliding hood. When you tighten the collet nut, the neoprene O-ring creates constant pressure on the hood and nut to prevent slippage and loosening.

112 BUYING NEW WADERS

When buying new waders, hip boots, or other wading or heavy boots, do so at the end of the day. That is when your feet swell, making an accurate measurement easier. Also, wear the socks that you would normally wear for fishing. Some anglers wear two pairs of regular socks, some a single pair of very heavy wool socks, and some a pair of medium wool socks over lightweight cotton socks.

This is important, even if buying boots by mail order. In that case, put on the appropriate socks at the end of the day, stand on paper on a hard floor, and have someone else trace around your foot. Send this tracing to the mail-order company or use its instructions to convert this information to the correct size. Often the best fit is a half- or full-size larger in a boot than you wear in a dress shoe.

"Fly-fishers fail in preparing their bait so as to make it alluring in the right quarter, for want of a due acquaintance with the subjectivity of fishes."

—George Eliot

The Mill on the Floss (1860)

113 LEARNING SIMPLE KNOTS

It is far better to learn a few knots very, very well than to know all the knots in the knot book, but have difficulty tying most of them. For most fly fishing, you only need a few knots. These include the following:

• A simple arbor knot to attach the line to the reel.

• A loop added to a fly line for loop-to-loop connections.

• A nail knot for the line/leader connection, if you are not using the loop-to-loop method.

• A mono loop knot for leader ends (with loop-to-loop connections), such as the perfection loop knot, figure-eight loop knot, or surgeon's loop knot.

ARBOR KNOT

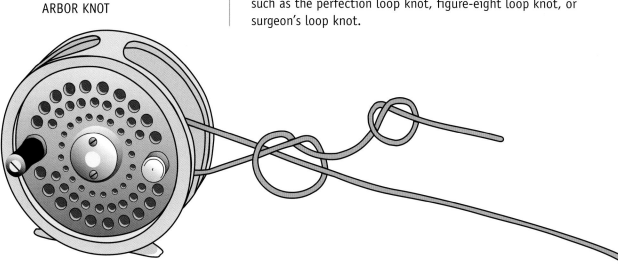

NAIL KNOT

LOOP TO LOOP CONNECTION

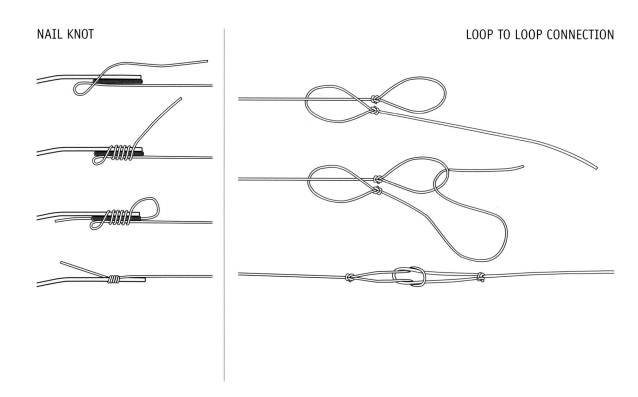

TACKLE AND TACKLE RIGGING

- A blood knot to make and retie leader sections.

- A fly-eye knot, such as a Palomar or improved clinch knot.

- A Bimini to make a long loop in your backing if not tying directly to the fly line.

If you do specialized fly fishing using wire or fishing the tropics, it also helps to know the following:

- A figure-eight knot for braided wire when fishing for toothy fish, such as bluefish, barracuda, and pike.

- An Albright, for tying a heavy bite leader to a light tippet section or backing to a fly line.

- A Homer Rhode loop knot for tying heavy bite mono to a fly.

PERFECTION LOOP

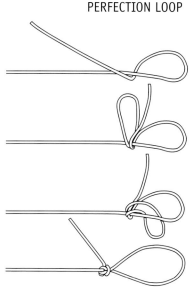

BLOOD KNOT

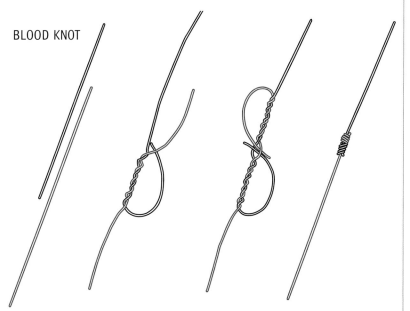

IMPROVED CLINCH KNOT

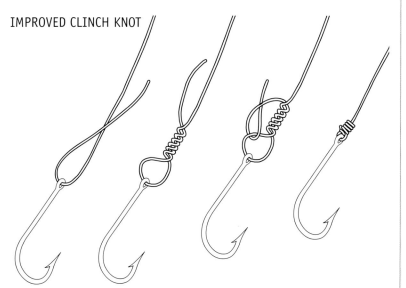

ALBRIGHT KNOT

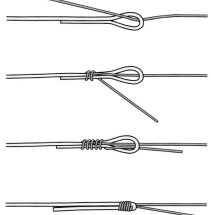

Chapter 4

General Fly Fishing

Tips for Essential Gear & Clothing

114 LEADER CAUGHT IN REEL

Leader ends are often caught in a reel under the line or other leader coils. To find the end of the leader (the leader tippet), use a hook (a large fly works well) to catch one leader coil. Then hold the fly with the leader coil and turn the reel handle as you would if retrieving line. The leader tippet will come free after a few turns.

115 WEIGHTED FLIES AND LEADER

Another situation that requires a change in casting tactics when surface fishing with a floating line occurs when you are casting heavily weighted flies. Common in steelhead and some trout fishing, this is often called a "chuck 'n duck" method of fishing, because of the problem of the heavy weight in the fly or leader tippet.

To help prevent problems, cast with a wide loop to keep the fly higher than normal and less dangerous to the caster. The necessity of these techniques varies with the weight in the fly or on the leader and also the size of the outfit and weight of the line.

116 TOUGH WADING SITUATIONS

In tough wading situations, it helps to have a buddy. If you have trouble getting across a certain stretch of river, two anglers can lock arms, take baby steps, and get across by supporting each other and providing additional resistance to the current. This is true whether or not you use a wading staff. It is even better if you both have wading staffs. For the safest wading, each angler alternates steps for wading so that one provides a solid "anchor" for the other as he or she moves.

117 FISH WITH A BUDDY WHEN WADING

It's always best to wade with a buddy, whether wet wading, in hip boots, or in chest-high waders. You and your friend should be within sight and earshot of each other. This is particularly true on big water. It is good to have a friend around for help in netting a fish or taking a photo of a trophy catch, but also for safety. Wading can wrench ankles, get you wet, cause you to fall in, or cause other problems; having a buddy around to help is both sensible and safe.

118 PREVENTING LINE TANGLES

Even after securing a fly to the hook keeper or to the guide, you still have a long length of line or leader from the tip-top to the reel seat. To prevent this from tangling with other rods or other tackle when storing gear, hold the line or leader in the middle and flip it around the rod, and over the nearest guide. This holds the line/leader out of the way, prevents it from hanging down, and keeps tangles to a minimum. Just remember that you did this so that you unhook the middle of the line/leader when getting the outfit ready to cast.

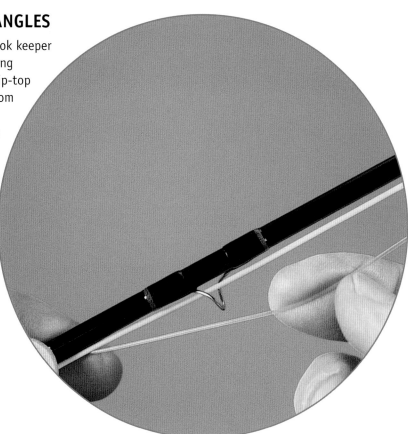

119 ANKLE SUPPORT

Boot-foot waders are easier to put on and take off and easier to travel with than separate wading shoes and stocking-foot waders. But for the best ankle support, the high top, heavy-leather wading shoes teamed with stocking-foot waders are best. If you have weak ankles, have broken or badly strained/sprained an ankle, or are fishing over very rough bottom, strongly consider these separate wader and wading shoe combinations.

120 SUN GLOVES

With more and more concern about skin cancer from the sun, anglers should consider wearing sun gloves while fishing. These are thin gloves with exposed fingertips (for tying knots and handling flies) that protect the backs of your hands from the damaging UV rays of the sun.

121 POLARIZING SUNGLASSES

Polarizing sunglasses allow you to see through the surface and also prevent glare. By reducing water surface glare, they prevent eyestrain and make fishing easier and more pleasant. By allowing you to see under the water surface, they allow spotting fish, structure, bottom, and currents. All will improve your fishing and help you to catch more fish.

122 VIEW WITH POLARIZING SUNGLASSES

Polarizing lenses in sunglasses prevent glare and allow you to see under the water, but they are dependent upon the angle with which the sun or sun reflection off of the water hits your glasses. Sometimes, you can improve this by slightly moving or angling your head to one side or the other to improve the polarizing angle for a better view beneath the surface. Do this frequently when trying to see fish or structure underwater.

123 DIFFERENT POLARIZING SUNGLASSES FOR DIFFERENT FISHING

When fly fishing in bright sun, use dark-lens polarizing sunglasses. Glasses with gray, copper, or brown lenses all have maximum protection and minimum light transmission of from 12 to 17 percent. Blue/gray is often best for offshore and open-water fishing; brown or copper for general fishing. These are best for bright sun and open water. For dim-light conditions use yellow lenses. These provide good contrast and are best for spotting fish. Transmission for these is about 25 to 32 percent. If fishing in both bright and dim conditions use two different pairs of sunglasses for the different light conditions.

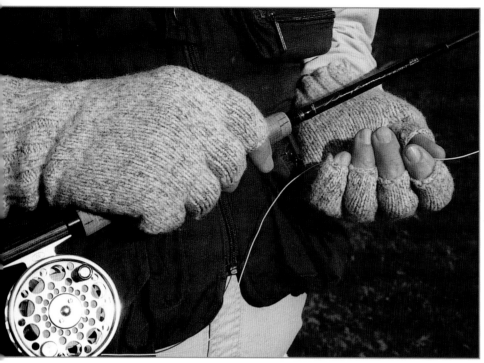

124 FINGERLESS GLOVES

Gloves of wool or heavy yarn synthetics are best for warmth when cold-weather fly fishing. The best of these have exposed fingers (fingerless gloves) so that you can handle flies, tie knots, prepare leaders, etc., while fishing without removing your gloves. Alternatives are mittens that have a covered palm opening to allow extending your fingers for tying knots and working with flies.

125 SUN SAFETY

If you are out in the hot sun all the time, tropical fishing, or have very sensitive light skin, consider "Lawrence of Arabia" headgear for your fly fishing. Several companies make caps or hats with an attached, roll-out neck protector, just as you see in films of Lawrence of Arabia and the French Foreign Legion. While sunscreen is good, these neck shields provide extra protection for the back of the neck and ears during a long day outdoors.

If you can't find or don't want to buy this specialized head gear you can accomplish the same thing with a standard fishing cap and handkerchief. Use several small safety pins to attach one edge of the handkerchief to the back rim of the cap. For emergency use when you don't have pins, place the handkerchief on the back of your head and carefully place the cap over it to hold it in place. Just don't take your cap off while fishing—you might lose your handkerchief.

126 TIPPET CHECK

After every catch, check your tippet for abrasion or roughness. Lightly run the leader tippet through your fingers, run it over your tongue, or hold it up to the light to spot any rough areas. Check particularly close to the fly. If you find a rough area, cut back the leader tippet if the roughness is close to the fly or replace the entire tippet to retie the fly.

127 THE LAST CAST

Whenever you reel in line to move to a new fishing location or at the end of the day, hold the rod tip in the water or against something solid such as a bush, a mossy bank, boat deck, etc. The reason is that without this support, the line can sometimes tangle around the rod tip, requiring time to untangle or even breaking the end of the rod. With the rod tip in the water, sometimes you can even get a strike on that last cast.

128 RELEASING FISH

Once you have caught a fish, taken a couple of quick photos, and unhooked it, you have to release it the right way if not keeping it. Don't just throw the fish into the water. Gently place the fish in the water. If it lacks teeth (trout, bass, stripers, carp, etc.), hold it by the lower jaw and work the fish back and forth to force water through the gills to help it to recover. Usually, the fish will dart out of your hand when it is ready to go.

If the catch has teeth, hold it in back of the head—just behind the gills—and by the tail. Work the fish back and forth to help it recover. With all fish, avoid dangerous parts of the fish (gills, pectoral spines, etc.) and wait for the fish to recover enough to dart out of your hand.

129 KEEPING COOL

In the hot sun, one way to keep cool is to wet your hat so that the evaporation cools your head as you fish. Some cap brims are only stiff cardboard, so wet only the cloth head covering part. If you are fishing in saltwater, use water from the cooler, since caps dipped in saltwater get sticky, stiff, and uncomfortable. Another way to keep cool is to slip an ice cube or two under your cap.

130 HAT UNDERBRIM

A hat or cap with a light underbrim bounces sunlight reflected from the water surface back into your eyes. A dark brim absorbs the light, which prevents eyestrain. This is true of any fishing, anywhere, for any species. You can even coat a favorite hat underbrim with black shoe polish or permanent black felt-tip marker.

"Fishermen are born honest, but they get over it."

—Ed Zern

To Hell with Fishing (1945)

131 HEAVY SHOCK LEADERS

If you use a heavy shock leader of mono tied with a clinch knot against the fly, the fly may have little action as a result of the stiff mono. To give the fly action, use a loop knot. The best is the Homer Rhode loop knot, which is simple to tie with heavy mono. It does not have the best knot strength, but when used with a heavy shock or bite leader, this makes no difference. The advantage is that the fly can swing, swim, twitch, and suspend independently of the heavy mono bite leader to have maximum action in the water.

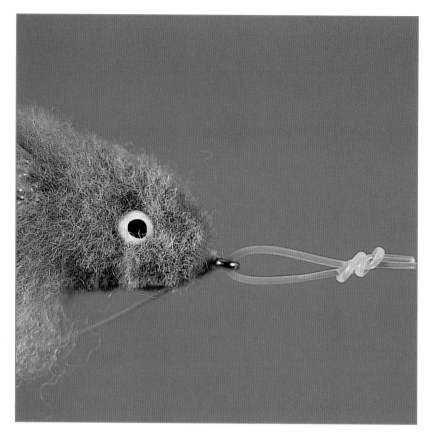

132 BRAIDED WIRE

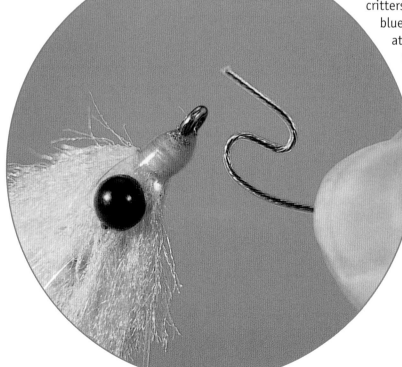

You need wire leaders when fishing for toothy critters, such as pike, muskie, barracuda, bluefish, and the like. An easy way to attach a fly to a braided wire leader is to thread the wire through the fly eye, then around the wire and back through the formed loop in the opposite direction. Tighten by pulling the tag end of the wire. This also makes it easy to replace flies, since you can back out the tag end, remove the fly, add a new fly, and repeat the tie without cutting the knot. Just make sure that you use this only with standard braided wire.

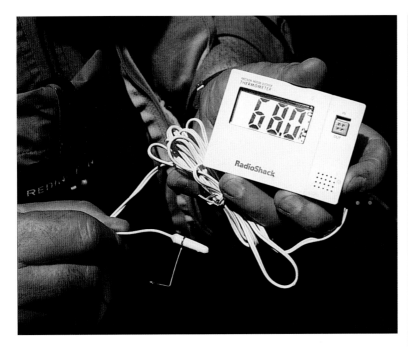

134 ELECTRIC TEMPERATURE GAUGE

Capt. Norm Bartlett, an expert and experienced captain on the Chesapeake Bay, but also an avid freshwater fly fisherman, came up with the idea of using a simple digital indoor/outdoor thermometer to check both water and ambient temperature while fishing. The length of thin cable for the outside measurement makes it possible to allow the thermocouple to drag in the water while you are wading, or to hang over the side while boat fishing. The length of the cable allows both deep and surface temperature readings. To get deep readings, carry a 1-ounce (28-g) sinker on a snap that you can fasten to the cord at the thermocouple to sink the probe. Regardless of how used, it can give instant temperature readings. A slide switch makes it possible to instantly check both air and water temperature, and most of them even allow switching between Fahrenheit and centigrade readings.

133 BELT YOUR WADERS

Many waders today include a belt that fits around your waist outside of the waders. This is for safety, since if you fall in, it reduces the amount of water that seeps into your waders. If your waders do not have this, buy a nylon belt or make one from nylon strapping and some snaps or Swedish buckles that allow for instant on/off of the belt. Buy 3 feet (0.9 m) or more (check your waist size with the waders on) of 1-inch (2.5-cm) nylon strapping and mating plastic snaps. Sew one end of the strapping to one snap and thread the other end through the two openings on the other snap. Tighten the belt around your waist anytime you wear waders.

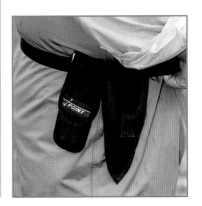

"There is no use in your walking five miles to fish when you can depend on being just as unsuccessful near home."

—Mark Twain (1835-1910)

135 SEAMS AND EDGES

Seams and edges are places where two currents touch, where two different flows of water meet, or where a fast current slides past a quiet eddy. Places like this in both freshwater and saltwater are ideal spots to throw a fly. They offer quiet water where game fish can rest while staying close to fast water that can wash a meal past their nose. For this reason, try fishing in the fast or faster current right next to the seam to get fish that are resting but ambush feeding. To produce the most strikes, cast the fly upcurrent and then allow it to swing downstream or down current on a snug line.

136 SPARE PLASTIC GARBAGE BAGS

Carry some spare plastic garbage bags with you on any fishing trip and keep one or two in a back pocket of your fishing vest. In an emergency, you can punch three holes in them for your head and arms to make an emergency rain jacket. They are also ideal to have on hand when you get back to the car to hold any wet or muddy waders, boots, socks, etc., and keep it separate from the rest of your tackle and the clean vehicle.

137 WADING STAFFS

Wading staffs are great when you need them and a nuisance when you don't. You need them when you get too deep into a stream, get into fast water, or are carrying a camera. Other times, they are in the way and can be a problem if you trip on them. The easy solution is to carry a folding wading staff in a holster on your wader belt. Several are available on the market now, varying in lengths to suit any angler.

The big advantage of these is that they all have an internal bungee cord so that by simply pulling the staff out of the holster by the handle, the rest of the wading staff springs and locks into a sturdy staff. The sections will not stay joined if the tip of the staff gets stuck in the mud, but that is a minor inconvenience.

138 IMPROVING WEED GUARDS

If you have a weed guard that is still catching weeds, there is a way to improve it and strengthen it for better weed protection. For the single mono-strand loops that are standard on most weedless flies and bugs, slip the weed guard around and in front of the hook bend. This effectively makes it stiffer. It repels weeds better and yet still collapses when a fish hits it.

139 PUMPING THE ROD

Non-anglers often wonder how an angler can land a heavy fish using a light tippet. The answer is in both the drag and the ability to pump, which is how to fight fish properly. First, the drag must be set much lighter than the pound-test of the leader. To fight fish properly with the fly rod (or any rod), bring the fish toward you by lifting the rod from the horizontal to about a 45-degree angle. Then lower the rod as you reel or strip in your fly line. Continue to do this until you land the fish or until it makes a run and you have to repeat the process. This also allows dropping the rod and allowing the line to run off of the fly reel, should the fish make a run while you are pumping it in. Note that it is also possible to work the rod with side pressure by working the rod back when held parallel to the water, then retrieving line with your hand or reel as you point the rod toward the fish each time.

140 PINCH DOWN HOOK BARB

The barbs on hooks designed to keep fish from becoming unbuttoned are not as important as we think. To make unhooking fish easy, pinch the barbs down with pliers. Use a flat-nose pliers held in line or on the axis with the hook point. This also makes it quick and easy to remove a fly should you hook yourself or a companion. Realize also that some fly fishing areas have regulations that require fishing only with barbless hooks. Check your local regulations for this to avoid problems.

141 CARRYING ROD

When walking through the woods or high grasslands with a fly rod tip first, you can easily poke the tip into a twig or brush and snap it before you realize it. To prevent this, pull the line and leader tight against the rod and carry the rod butt forward with the rod trailing behind you. In most cases, the rod will clear all of the brush and foliage, but, if the rod does catch, it is easy to untangle without damage.

142 CLEANING FISHING AREAS

One way to help control angler litter is to carry a plastic trash bag with you and use it to pick up litter around boat ramps, shore fishing areas, and along streams. Since most anglers walk in one direction along a stream to fish it and then walk back to return to the car, use the bag on the return trip to pick up any litter that you have encountered. Carry the trash home to dispose of it properly.

143 COUNT DOWN FISHING

A great way to fly fish for deep fish is to use the "count down" method. This involves using a sinking fly and sinking or sinking-tip fly line, and counting down with each successive cast. By counting, you are essentially "timing" the sink rate of your fly. Counting "one thousand one, one thousand two," etc., makes for a reasonable count in seconds. By making such a count after each cast and before a retrieve, and increasing the count by one or two with each successive cast, you can determine the correct count to strike fish at a certain depth. Once you hook a fish, use the count to get to the same level in the water column to take fish during subsequent casts.

144 YO-YO LIFT

Natural nymphal forms of insects, such as caddis, mayflies, and stoneflies, live on the bottom of a stream. At the end of their life cycle, they rise to the surface, emerge from the water, and develop into winged insects. With different species, this occurs all the time, almost all year round.

To capitalize on this, fish nymphs deep on trout streams and use your rod to lift the nymph up; then allow it to fall to the bottom again as it drifts downstream.

This method of nymph fishing, popularized by Jim Leisenring some 65 years ago, is still an effective way to fish today, since it closely simulates the movement of nymphs swimming to the surface. For best results, use a weighted nymph or some split shot on the leader tippet to keep the nymph deep.

146 WADING METHODS

Wade sideways to the current to create less water pressure against you than you would if facing the current. Wade slowly and plant one foot firmly before moving your other foot. This prevents mishaps from rolling rocks, slippery ledges, and eroding gravel bars. Also, use a wading staff with the staff on the up-current side of the river so that you can lean into the current. This is generally better than using the wading staff down current where it might slip and cause you to fall or allow the current to push you down.

145 FIGHTING BIG FISH

Since you strip fly line out to cast, you can fight fish in two ways: stripping them in or fighting them from the reel. It's best to leave this decision—strip or reel—to the fish. If a fish is small and you can strip it in, do so without reeling in line at the same time. Often anglers trying to reel in line while stripping in a fish at the same time end up losing the fish. If the fish is strong and makes a run, allow the line to run controlled (through your fingers) out of the guides until all the slack line is gone. At this point, drop the rod tip a little and push the rod toward the fish to lessen the shock of the fish pulling line from the reel and against the drag. Then fight the fish from the reel—reeling it in by pumping when the fish tires, and allowing the fish to run when it desires.

"No matter how long an angler does it, fly fishing remains an endless, delightful surprise. That's what we love about it.... To people who don't study a river's face to learn what is in its heart, or turn over riverbed rocks to find the life beneath them, or see the image of a mayfly in little pieces of birds and critters attached to a hook, the whole game must seem a frivolous exercise in chance. To we who enjoy this sport, the mysteries make perfect sense. We can count on being surprised. That's reason enough to go back to the water."

—Art Scheck

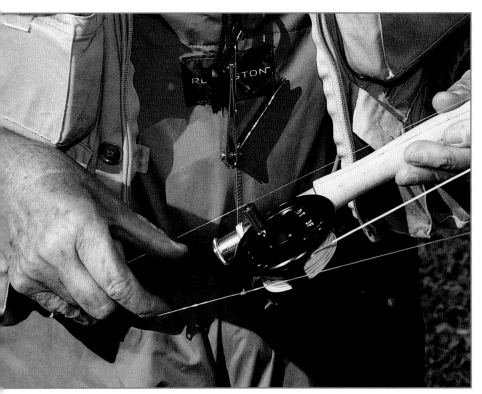

147 LOOPING LONG LEADER

Most anglers fly fish with a long leader—longer than the length of the fly rod. If you slip the fly into the hook keeper and reel the leader through the rod tip, it creates a sharp bend or kink in the butt section of the leader. To prevent this, and keep the line and leader secured, keep the end of the fly line several inches out of the rod tip, hook the fly into one of the upper guides, and loop the extra leader around the circumference of the reel. This allows using the rod instantly, since you do not catch the leader/line connection in the tip-top.

148 FLY FISHING DEEP

The right way to fly fish deep in open water is with a sinking line. While sinking-tip lines are great, the floating portion tends to plane up the sinking-tip end and raise the fly in the water column. To get down and stay down, use a full-sinking line, add a "mini lead head" between the line and the leader, use a short leader, and keep the rod tip low throughout the retrieve. This keeps your fly in the deep strike zone from the moment the fly sinks after making the cast until you pull the line out of the water for the next cast.

149 TIPPET SIZE

One way to minimize drag in any fly fishing situation is to use a very long, fine tippet. Make sure that you are using very flexible tippet and leader material that can drift with the current and not stiffen to cause the fly to drag. By using a long tippet, you have the maximum flexibility possible to prevent drag from affecting the fly. By using the finest tippet you dare, you have minimal possible chance of the fish sighting your leader or you and the maximum flexibility in the tippet section.

This same solution applies when sight-fishing in very shallow water for fish like bonefish and permit and on some clear river trout situations.

150 LOOP CONTROL

Over the years, anglers have suggested several ways to hold coils of line to prevent the current from catching it when wade fishing, or to keep boat fittings from catching the line. One of the best ways is to hold each coil of line on a separate finger of your line hand as you strip in the line. This allows you to carry four large coils of line in your hand without any possibility of them tangling, as might occur if looping coils together in the palm of your hand. This also makes it easy to release the line without tangling when making the next cast or shooting line.

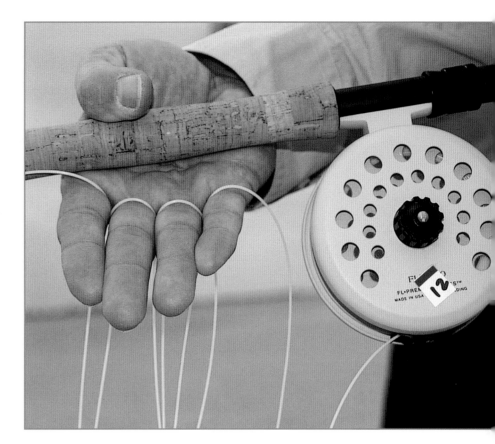

151 CLOTHING FOR FISHING

Most fishing vests are tan, gray, or green. You will seldom find large blocks of one solid color in nature, and such vests might spook trout in shallow-water streams. To camouflage yourself while fishing, wear a camouflage shirt or lightweight jacket, similar to what hunters wear. But for best results, wear the jacket *over* your fishing vest to disguise and hide that solid color. You can leave the jacket open in front to easily get flies and other necessities from your pockets, while the mixed pattern of the jacket or shirt hides you from the trout.

Choose the pattern of camouflage to match the woods where you will be fishing. Available camouflages include spring woods, fall trees, large trees, winter with snow, barren areas, etc. Best for most early-season trout fishing would be a spring (green pattern) woods look.

152 SINK LEADERS WITH MUD

If your leaders are not sinking, and creating refraction on the surface to scare trout, use mud to sink the monofilament. Smear the mud along the entire length of the leader to help it soak up water (it will absorb water in time anyway) and sink on the next cast.

153 DRYING FLIES

It is important to dry flies after use before placing them in a closed fly box. A simple way to do this is to make a fly-drying box for small flies. I first learned of this when fishing in Pennsylvania and a thoughtful fly angler gave me one.

This fly-drying box is nothing more than a plastic film can, with two large "windows" cut into the sides. The liner of the can is a small piece of plastic screening (available at any hardware store as a "patch" piece), coiled, and cut to fit inside the can to prevent fly loss. A cord loop through a hole punched in the side of the can, then through the lid, back through the lid and into the other side allows the can to hang from your vest while preventing loss of the cap. The screening allows flies to dry as you fish.

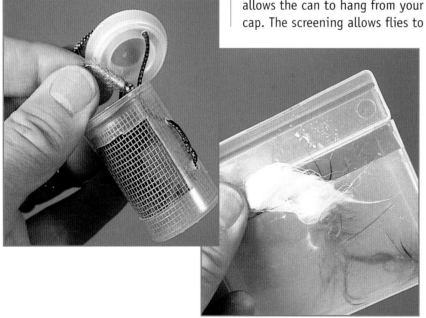

For larger flies or different fishing situations, place all used flies in a bag or box for later drying. If fishing in saltwater, rinse the flies in fresh water at home, dry thoroughly, and replace them in their boxes. A simple container can be anything, including a zipper-seal plastic bag, plastic zippered pencil case (such as can be used for storage of large flies), or any of a number of small plastic boxes (such as Tupperware or pencil case boxes).

154 RIFFLING HITCH

The riffling hitch is a simple hitch of the leader tippet around the head of the fly that causes the fly to skitter over the surface, often taking large fish. It was designed for Atlantic salmon fishing, but you can use the riffling hitch for any fishing where you want to attract big fish to the surface.

To make the riffling hitch, first tie the tippet to the head of the fly with any standard knot. Then form a half-hitch loop in the end of the tippet and loop this over the head of the fly so that it tightens and grips the fly immediately in back of the head. Make a second half-hitch loop to secure the tippet to the head. You can make this so that the leader tippet is on the right side or the left side of the fly, depending upon whether you want the fly skittering to the right or the left.

155 ANOTHER WAY TO SINK LEADERS

Another way to sink leaders is to take a tip from the past when fly anglers used to carry their silk gut leaders in aluminum cases between layers of wet felt to keep them moist and ready for casting. Manufacturers designed this to help the silk leaders straighten out easily. Store your leaders in a zipper-seal sandwich bag with a few drops of water that the leader will absorb. This allows the leader to sink quickly when fishing and prevents the leader from floating and scaring fish. It also makes it easier to straighten the leader.

156 SINKING LINES

Sinking lines and long-section sinking-tip fly lines are thinner than comparable-weight floating lines and thus have a different mass/air resistance ratio. As a result, it is better to cast through a greater angle with the rod to create a wider loop to prevent line tangles. This wide loop keeps the parts of the line separate so that the weighted line does not fall on itself and tangle.

Chapter 5

Casting

From Line Control to Mending to Retrieving

157 CONTROLLING LINE LOOP

Loop control of your line is a must if you are to fly fish effectively. In most cases, you will want a tight or small loop for pushing out a line for both distance and accuracy. In some cases, you need a wide loop, as when casting sinking lines or large, heavily weighted flies.

To control the loop size, control the angle of your rod on both the forward and backcast. To make a narrow loop, stop the rod power in a high position, following through only after you make that stop and to finish the cast. To cast a wide loop, continue through more of the cast than above to allow the loop to open more on the cast, and prevent tangles of weighted flies and sinking lines. Practice this often, first with a floating line and then with a sinking line until you understand the physics involved, the need for different types of casts, and the technique required to make them consistently.

158 RETRIEVE AS SOON AS FLY HITS WATER

Some fish do not react well if a fly lands but does not move immediately. This applies to barracuda, among others. For fish like this, cast, but begin your retrieve just as soon as the fly hits the water to attract any fish in the area. Barracuda usually lose interest in the fly if cast and not moved immediately.

159 CASTING WITH EITHER HAND

To become a better angler, learn to cast with either hand. One easy way to do this is to hold the rod with both hands while allowing your dominant hand to control the cast. This "teaches" your other hand and arm the mind/muscle memory that is so necessary to perform any manual task well. In time, gradually allow your other hand to share the casting stroke with your dominant hand, then allow your non-dominant hand to take over as it learns to cast well. With this skill, you will be able to make casts to both sides of structure (rocks if trout fishing, perhaps duck blinds if bass fishing) that you could not otherwise easily reach by casting with only one arm. For help in accomplishing this, try Capt. Norm Bartlett's Fly Casting Trainer. It is a separate handle that fits any rod grip to allow your rod hand to teach through mind/muscle memory the correct action for your non-dominant hand.

"Here are a couple good tips: Wait out your backcast. Don't enter tournaments."

—Flip Pallot

160 RETRIEVING LINE

There are several good ways to retrieve fly line when stripping in flies. Each retrieve type has an advantage. By folding the line over repeatedly in your hand, you can keep the line snug with a drifting or slow retrieve. This is ideal for fishing nymphs. For faster stripping of streamer flies, retrieve the line so that you can hold coils in your hand. If fishing from a boat, you can strip the line onto the casting deck, but do not step on the line when making the next cast or when a hooked fish makes a run.

161 SWINGING THE FLY

One of the most effective retrieve systems for running water is to make a cast across the current or stream, and then allow the fly to swing in an arc through the current until it is straight downstream. This is a classic cast and retrieve system for Atlantic salmon, Pacific salmon, shad, stripers, trout, river smallmouth, and other game fish.

To completely cover the water in a long pool, make one or two such casts, and then make a large side step downstream and repeat. This allows the fly to swing through a new section of water a foot or two (30 to 60 cm) below the first cast. By repeating this regularly, you can easily cover an entire pool.

162 LANDING PIKE

Pike have teeth and you can't lip them as you can largemouth bass. An old way to land pike was to put your thumb and forefinger into their pronounced eye sockets and lift them into the boat. Don't do it! In these days of catch-and-release fishing, such mistreatment can damage or possibly blind the fish, dooming it to a slow death. Instead, use a cradle (square net) to land pike.

To make a cradle, buy a rectangle of mesh netting, about 3 feet by 4 feet (0.9 m by 1.2 m). (You can make it smaller or larger depending upon the fish you plan to catch.) Then staple or stitch the long side of the net to 1½-inch (38-mm) dowels, 5 feet (1.5 m) long, to the dowel. It will look almost like a World War II stretcher or a camp cot. To help sink the netting, add a few small pinch-on sinkers along the net. To land the pike, suspend the cradle in the water to sink the netting. Have the angler lead the pike into the cradle. Then lift both sides of the cradle to lift the pike straight up to remove the fly and release the fish.

163 FALSE CASTING

Shallow-water fish are particularly susceptible to being spooked when a fly line is cast over them. This is particularly true of trout and saltwater flats species, such as bonefish and permit. To prevent this when false casting, cast to the side of the fish to get the right distance and then only on the final cast make the cast toward the target. This lessens the possibility of the line scaring the fish.

164 CASTING WITH THE WIND FROM THE RIGHT

For right-handed casters, a wind from the right is the worst wind to deal with. To prevent hooking yourself or others, you have two choices. One is to turn 180 degrees and cast so that your rod arm is on the far side of the wind. For this, make several false casts and then on the final forward cast, turn back 180 degrees to push the line toward the target.

An alternative is to keep the wind to your right, but cast with the rod angled over your left shoulder to keep the line from blowing back in your face. Since the wind will tend to blow the fly off target, you might have to compensate by casting slightly into the wind so that the fly lands in the target area.

In all cases, make sure that you are not casting where you might hook other anglers. If you are left-handed, follow the directions for casting with the wind from the left.

165 CASTING WITH THE WIND

The wind does not always have to be the enemy when fly casting. If casting with the wind direction, use the wind to get a longer cast. To do this, make a forceful side backcast as low as possible and parallel to the water. Then at the end of the backcast, swing the rod to a vertical position to make a high overhead forward cast with a wide loop. The wind will catch the loop and give you more distance than you often get on a calm day.

166 CASTING INTO THE WIND

Casting into the wind is more difficult than casting with the wind. To do this, make all casts to the side, low and parallel to the water, to keep the line trajectory low and lessen the force of the wind on the line. An alternative is to make a high overhead backcast, then a strong, forceful low forward cast with a narrow loop to drive the line low and into the wind. The low forward cast will push the line under the most forceful part of the wind to get the fly out to the target.

167 CASTING WITH THE WIND FROM THE LEFT

If right-handed, the wind from the left will blow the line away from you and not cause a danger to you or anglers to the left of you. You can still make overhead or side casts, but must compensate for the wind blowing the fly off target. Thus, cast slightly into the wind direction.

In all cases, make sure that you are not casting where you might hook other anglers. If you are left-handed, follow the directions for casting with the wind from the right.

168 SIDE ROLL CAST

Use roll casts where there is no room for a traditional backcast. Traditionally, anglers make roll casts straight overhead, like hammering a nail. A better way to make them is with a side cast, bringing the rod back, pausing, and then casting forward parallel with the water to roll the line out to the quarry. This works better, is easier, and allows for a longer cast than a traditional roll cast.

> *"I fish all the time when I'm at home; so when I get a chance to go on vacation, I make sure I get in plenty of fishing."*
>
> —Thomas McGuane
>
> *"Fishing the Big Hole"*
>
> *An Outside Chance* (1990)

170 REMOVING HOOKS FROM YOU OR FRIENDS

If you fish long enough, you might get hooked or be in a fishing group where someone gets hooked. If this happens with a barbed hook that penetrates past the barb, you can't back the hook out of the flesh. After some barbaric methods of the past (push the hook out through the skin, cut off the barb and then back the hook out!) the best current method recommends pulling the hook out backward using a loop of string.

For this, first cut the fly from the tippet. Then use cord or a heavy fly line looped around the hook bend of the fly. Push down on the eye of the fly hook and then jerk the fly out backward with the loop of cord by pulling on the bend of the hook. If you have antiseptic, add it to the puncture, and cover the spot with a bandage. This is easiest (and sometimes only possible) if someone other than the "hookee" does it. This works well for all areas of the body, but avoid doing this around the neck, face, back of hands, or anywhere that you might have surface arteries, veins, nerves, or tendons.

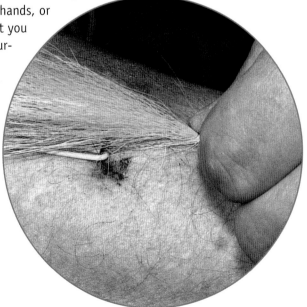

169 CASTING SINKING FLY LINES

The best way to cast a sinking fly line after retrieving the line all the way back is to make an aerial roll cast. Since the line is deep, it is impossible to pick the line up off the water as you can with a floating line. Instead, wait until you have only about 15 feet (4.6 m) of line out. Then bring the rod back and roll the sinking line out of the water and into the air. Make this a high, aerial roll cast to prevent casting the line out on the water again. Once the line straightens out in the air, bring the line back in a backcast and make the few necessary false casts to get the line out again.

171 HIGH BACKCAST

"Backcast" is probably a poor word to use for the technique of flipping the line back in preparation for the forward cast and retrieving the fly. Often, beginning fly anglers bring the rod back too far and at too much of an angle so that the line hits the water. This reduces the power of loading the rod for the forward cast and also often makes for a high, jerky, forward cast.

To make a good cast, make a high backcast, with enough power to keep a straight line, then come forward to power the forward cast. This ensures that the line will stay high and make a good casting technique. Another problem with a low or angled backcast on small streams is that you can hit and break off your fly on rocks in back of you.

172 MENDING LINE

One way to get more drift to a fly is to "mend" the line. Mending the line is a method of flipping the line upstream to prevent it from dragging downstream by the current and developing a belly to race the fly through the water where it will be unattractive to fish. To mend line after the cast, tighten the line slightly, hold the line and rod, point the rod tip toward the line direction, and flip the rod in an upward arc to cause the line belly to flip upstream and give the fly more natural drift time.

173 DOUBLE-HAUL

The double-haul is a little like learning to pat your tummy while rubbing your head—or is it the other way around? The double-haul is a way to accelerate and speed up your line to make good casts and to get more distance when required.

To make the double-haul, first pick up the line for the backcast by pulling on the line while raising the rod to make the backcast. Then, as the backcast forms, hold the line but allow a short length of it to slide through the guides. Allow the backcast to straighten out. Then pull forward on the line to accelerate it while pushing the rod forward to make the forward cast. This combination of pulling on the line while pushing the rod forward accelerates the line to make long casts possible and easier.

174 RETRIEVE ROUTE THROUGH WEEDS

Surface pads of weeds, or even patches of weeds, such as lily pads, spatterdock, water hyacinth, etc., can make fishing a popping bug or slider difficult. Even with a weedless bug, it is difficult to get through such weeds. One way around this is to use a 9-foot (2.7-meter) rod and "plan" a route for your bug before you make a cast. The reason for the long rod is that it allows you to position the rod to the right or left as you zigzag the bug through the open water path between the weeds. Of course, this is not possible on all waters, or on completely weed-choked waters, but is possible where you have enough open water to snake a bug through these patches of bass-holding cover.

176 CASTING FROM SHORE

If you can cast effectively from shore, don't wade. Wading is important but also can create bottom noise, make ripples and pressure waves that spook fish, and create the potential of falling or slipping. If you can cast from the bank and get to the fish, do it. For this, use a standard overhead cast if you are in field or meadow situations, or use a standard or side roll cast if you are on a tree-lined bank.

175 LINE CONTROL ON RETRIEVES

When retrieving a fly, make sure that you never completely let go of the line. Hold the rod in your rod hand and run the line over your index finger. Then make the twitches, jerks, pauses, strips, and other retrieve moves with your line hand, pulling the line through the index finger of your rod hand. That way, when you drop the line with your line hand to reposition it for the next strip, you still have control of the line through your opposite index finger. This also allows you to strike a fish, should one hit during this transition moment. Do this by tightening the index finger of your rod hand, then picking up the line with your line hand to fight the fish.

177 CONTROLLING FISH

If you pressure a hooked fish with a high rod, it tends to come to the surface, thrash around, and possibly become unbuttoned. A better solution is to use side pressure with the rod held close to parallel with the water. This tends to keep the fish in the water rather than struggling on top, and allows you to turn the head of the fish to lead it to you.

178 CASTING SINKING SHOOTING HEADS

You must cast sinking shooting heads, such as the Teeny lines, those by other manufacturers, or those that you make yourself, differently than regular fly lines. First, shooting heads or lines are usually about 30 feet (9 m) long, and typically attached to a running line with a loop-to-loop system. Loops are typically included on commercial lines, or you can make your own by whipping a folded-over loop in the end of the line (see page 38). The running line looped to the shooting head is typically a thin, level fly line or a special braided shooting line, such as Gudebrod 25- or 35-pound-test (11.3- or 15.9-kg) Shooting Line, that is a bright-orange braided mono.

To cast a shooting line, work the shooting head outside of the tip of the fly rod so that as you double-haul, you are working the end of the shooting line back and forth. You do not want to pull the connecting loops back and forth through the tip-top. Double-haul as you keep the line in the air, and make wide loops with your rod angle control. Once you have made a few false casts, double-haul, and shoot the line to the target, allowing the stiff shooting line to flow up out of the stripping basket or off the boat deck. Since the shooting line flows through the guides faster and easier than any fly line, you achieve a far longer cast than one possible with a standard weight-forward fly line.

179 TIMING THE STRIKE

Timing is everything, particularly when it comes to striking fish. The best advice is to wait until you feel the fish to set the hook. This is true even if you see the pick-up of a bonefish when sight-fishing, or the boil of a bass when popping a surface bug. If you react to what you see, rather than what you feel, you can pull the fly out of the fish's mouth before it completely takes it. With a surface strike, allow the fish to turn with the bug or fly in its mouth before striking. On underwater pick-ups when sight-fishing, wait until the fish moves away or turns and you feel the weight of the fish.

180 BACKCASTING

If you rip the line off of the water for a backcast, you spook fish throughout the area. To prevent this, keep the rod tip low, strip in line until you are ready to cast, and then lift the rod until only the leader or part of the leader is on the water surface. Then (and only then) lever the rod back to make the backcast and raise the rest of the leader and the bug or fly off of the water. The result is a smooth, clean pick-up with minimal disturbance of the water surface for an easy backcast to get the fly or bug back out to waiting fish.

181 AERIAL ROLL CAST

If you fish long enough and in enough different places, weeds ultimately catch on your fly. One way to remove weeds without physically handling the fly is to strip the line in, and with the fly a dozen feet (3.7 m) from you, bring the rod back to make a roll cast. Then make a rapid aerial roll cast, throwing the line into the air prior to making a backcast. Make the backcast as soon as the line straightens out from the roll cast. Done right, this will often strip the weeds from the fly as you rip the fly out of the water or as the fly changes direction on the backcast. As you cast, check the fly in the air to make sure that it is clean and free of weeds.

182 CASTING EASE

There are fishing situations for both short rods and long rods, but as a general rule, long rods are better. With a long rod, you have more leverage to make longer casts. You also require less effort and muscle strain with long rods. They are better shock absorbers, since the longer the flexible lever (the rod) the less likely that the fish can snap the leader tippet.

Long rods are also good for "dapping," a technique of fishing with the tip of the rod dropping the line straight down to allow the fly to float on the water surface or, when nymphing, deep in the current. You do this without casting and without the line floating on the surface. You can poke long rods through the brush of a mountain trout stream to present a fly easily without casting. A light, short rod, however, might work better on some small meadow streams when throwing small terrestrials and tiny midge patterns.

183 WEAK BACKCAST

If you can't get weeds off of your fly by a rapid roll cast, or if you see a knot in your leader, the only way to correct this is to handle the line/leader and remove the weeds or untie and retie the knot. One way to rapidly do this is to pick up the line and make a very weak backcast over your left shoulder (assuming that you are a right-handed caster). Do this so that you can catch the leader as the line collapses just as it gets to you with this very weak backcast. Then with the leader in hand, untie or retie any knots, and clear the fly for the next cast.

184 SHOOT LINE ON THE BACKCAST

To get the maximum line speed—and thus distance—in your fly casting, you need to load your rod as much as possible to create kinetic (stored) energy that can kick out the fly line on the forward cast. For this, it helps to shoot line on the backcast, which then creates more bend or load in the rod for the forward cast.

To do this, make your normal single-haul backcast, but with a little more power than usual. Then allow the fly line to slip through your fingers as the line propels to the rear with the extra power that you put into the cast. Stop the fly line with the line still straight behind you, and then pull down on the line to create a double-haul as you push the rod forward for the forward cast. The result is a more heavily loaded rod that propels the line in a strong forward cast for maximum distance.

185 DISTANCE CASTS

Any athlete uses his or her entire body when performing their sport. The same thing applies to fly fishing, particularly when making distance casts. To make distance casts, use all of your arm and entire body to help punch out the line. Position your feet so that the foot opposite your rod hand is forward to give you balance when you make the cast. This is the same position that you would assume in throwing a baseball or swinging a tennis racket to get the maximum control and distance.

186 LIP LANDING LARGE FISH

Lip landing large fish, such as stripers, steelhead, and salmon, can be difficult. The fish are strong, with tremendous power to twist out of your grip and break tackle. Many fish, such as big largemouth, trout, steelhead, and salmon, also have small but abrasive teeth that can make you sore. One good tip for these situations is to use a rag or small towel. Wet it and hold it between your fingers, then lip-grab the fish by the towel held in your hand. This creates a better grip, is easier on the fish, and won't abrade your thumb. You can also use a cotton gardening or work glove for the same purpose.

187 CLEANING TROUT

There is a right way and wrong way to clean trout along a stream to take home for a meal. The right way is to first kill the trout with a sharp rap on the head or by inserting your thumb into the mouth (small trout only) and bending back the head against your index finger to break its neck. Then, once the fish is dead, use a fine-point knife to cut the fish from the vent to the gills. Remove the abdominal cavity contents and then tear or cut out the gills. Once you've done this, use your thumbnail to run along the backbone of the stomach cavity to remove the dark red line (the fish's kidneys). With the organs removed, lightly pack the stomach cavity with ferns or grass, wrap in grasses and store in the back pocket of your fishing vest until you can get to a cooler and ice.

Chapter 6

Freshwater Fly Fishing

Working Streams & Rivers

188 FIGURE-EIGHT BOAT RETRIEVE

One trick that pike and muskie anglers use to attract strikes from a following fish is to work the lure (often a big spoon) in several large figure-eight patterns next to the boat. This technique often infuriates pike or muskie into striking. You can do the same thing with a fly, working it in a figure-eight pattern close to the boat before you pick up the line for the next cast.

This requires several things, only applicable to pike and muskie fishing. One is that you retrieve the fly all the way to the boat to catch the followers that often occur with these species. The second is that you use a short leader—about 4 feet (1.2 m)—so that you have the end of the fly line outside of the tip-top when making these figure-eight patterns with your rod. This prevents tangles and breaks when a fish hits, which might occur if the line/leader connection were in the guides. The third is to use a 9-foot (2.7-meter) or longer fly rod to give you the leverage to work the fly in these "infinity" patterns. The fourth is that you have the line in a stripping basket or neatly coiled to prevent any tangles that can cause a break-off when the pike makes a run after striking.

189 TANDEM RIGS

At one time "casts" of three flies on a leader were standard—one on the "point" (the end of the leader) and two dropper flies above. Tandem rigs of two flies are still a good idea, since they give fish a choice of two offerings, and can greatly increase your chances of hooking up. Possibilities include two dries, two wets or nymphs, two streamers, or a combination, such as a nymph and a streamer or a subdued nymph and a bright wet fly.

190 DOWNSTREAM SWING

You can easily take some migrating fish by using the downstream swing. These are fish like shad, steelhead, and salmon (Atlantic and Pacific), which are anadromous and ascend streams to spawn. They often run through a riffle to rest at the tail end of a pool before moving on. To catch such fish, an ideal retrieve is to position yourself so that the fly line drifting straight downstream swings in the current where the fish are holding.

You can also benefit by causing the fly to swing back-and-forth. To do this, swing your rod to one side so that the current catches the belly of the line, and ultimately causes the fly to swing to one side. Then throw the rod to the other side where the current will catch the line belly again and cause the fly to swing back. This back-and-forth movement across the current at the tail of a pool often triggers fish to strike.

"*I consider him, inch for inch and pound for pound, the gamest fish that swims.*"

—James Henshall

Book of the Black Bass (1881)

191 READING THE WATER FOR LARGEMOUTH BASS

Studies have shown that largemouth bass like structure, particularly wood. Thus, the place to cast a fly or bug for largemouth bass is around any wood structure. Logjams, stumps, standing timber, wood piers or docks, brush piles, boathouses, duck blinds, and similar wood structure are ideal for shallow-water bass. If wood is not available in largemouth territory, then fish rocks or any other available structure.

The exceptions to the above occur in mid-summer and mid-winter when bass are deep along break lines, and in the summer and fall when they are cruising the shallows for food each morning and evening.

192 READING THE WATER FOR SMALLMOUTH BASS

While smallmouth bass seem similar to largemouth, smallmouth like structure of gravel or rock far better than the wood favored by largemouth. Thus, cast bugs and flies around boulders, rocks, ledges, shelves, gravel beds, and such on smallmouth rivers. Since they are often taking nymphs and hellgrammites from the bottom, another spot to try with large, black, weighted nymphs is to fish the bottom of sandy or gravel areas through deep, long pools. If rock is not available on smallmouth rivers, then fish wood or other available structure, since smallmouth adapt to any situation.

193 COPING WITH FALL LEAVES

Fall leaves floating on the surface or sinking in the water make two difficult situations when fall fly fishing. And there are two solutions. If the leaves are only floating on the surface, as during early in the season or on a windy day, use a very slow sinking line. Cast, twitch the fly line to get the line just barely under the water, and then retrieve the fly with the tip down and touching the water surface. The low tip and the slow sinking line keeps the floating leaves from interfering with the retrieve.

If the leaves are sinking, use the same technique, but with a floating line and floating, or weedless, fly to keep from catching the underwater leaves. In both cases it also helps to use a very slow retrieve to avoid sinking the hook into a leaf.

194 SPOTTING FRESHWATER FISH

You can spot different freshwater fish in different ways. Trout reveal themselves by rising to the surface to take insects. But you can also spot their flashes on the bottom as their bellies show when turning to search for nymphs. You can find carp and smallmouth in shallow waters rooting around rocks while searching for crayfish. They often travel together, each taking advantage of the other's food gathering methods.

Panfish, such as bluegills, often take bugs off the surface. In the springtime you'll find their round light-colored beds along the banks in shallow water. You'll find largemouth beds along the shore also, but they are larger and often found in very shallow water. Smallmouth have similar beds, but usually in deeper water.

Nervous water or any water during which you see baitfish moving or nervous can signal smallmouth, largemouth, or one of the pike or muskie families.

195 STRIKE INDICATOR

One way to use tandem rigs very effectively is to use a nymph on the end of the leader with a bushy dry fly about 18 inches (45.7 cm) up the leader. This dry fly can be on a dropper extension of the leader or tied to the end of the leader with an 18-inch length of tippet material connecting the nymph to the hook bend of the dry fly. This allows a fish to take either on top or down deep, and also allows the dry fly to serve as a strike indicator for the nymph.

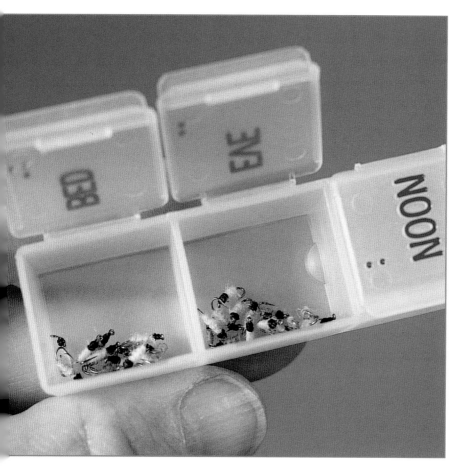

196 TYPES OF STRIKE INDICATORS

There are many types of strike indicators in addition to the dry fly. Possibilities include strike indicator yarn, small floats made for the purpose, floating putty that you can add to the leader, or fold-over adhesive foam pads. Often the best are those that are black or white (or both—for maximum visibility under any water conditions), so that they won't spook fish as might occur with bright colors. Strike indicators, regardless of type, are simply fishing floats or bobbers (although fly anglers do not like to think of them this way) and help you detect when a fish has taken a nymph or other underwater offering.

197 MORE STRIKE INDICATORS

An easy way to carry the yarn-style strike indicators is to get a long length of the yarn and shove it into a plastic 35-mm film can. Poke or drill a hole in the can lid, appropriate to the size of the yarn used. Keep a pair of scissors in your vest to clip the yarn, and remove only enough of the yarn needed for each application.

198 STORING SMALL FLIES

Small flies, size 18 and smaller, have a habit of getting lost, getting mixed up with other flies, or escaping from their compartments in standard fly boxes. To prevent this, use a special box for small flies. Actually, make up several boxes, since the best for these small flies are the individually lidded compartment pillboxes.

You can get two styles—one with four compartments for daily dosing, and one with seven compartments for weekly dosing. The big advantage is that each style of box has individual compartments with separate lids, and that lid has internal ridges around all four sides to prevent even the smallest flies from escaping. An added advantage of these is that with only one compartment open at a time, you are less likely to lose flies should you drop the box or the wind gusts unexpectedly.

199 WADING IN THE CURRENT

When wading a stream or river, it helps to shuffle your feet slightly. This allows you to use your moving foot to feel ahead of you for rocks, boulders, or smooth bottom, and also helps you maintain balance in fast water. Take care that you do not dislodge rocks while doing this, since it might affect your balance and also make some mudding downstream as rocks roll out from under you.

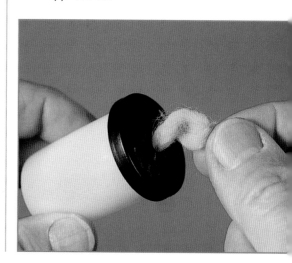

200 FLOATING FLIES

Many emerging flies (mayflies, caddis flies, and stone flies) float in the water film, rather than on top of it as do the mature dry spinner forms and the dry flies designed to imitate them. To simulate a struggling fly, take some of your darker colored dry flies and use scissors to trim along the bottom of the fly. That way, the tail, body, and hackle float in the surface, rather than riding high. In essence, you are taking standard dry flies to make them into flies that float in the surface film as do the specially designed comparaduns.

201 FRESHWATER FISH DANGERS

Catfish spines are very sharp and carry a toxic substance that can cause a painful, festering wound. To land a catfish up to about 5 pounds (2.3 kg), reach carefully around the sharp spines on the dorsal fin and pectoral fins. Grab the fish from the top by holding it with your hand immediately in back of the dorsal fin and the index and middle finger bracketing one pectoral fin.

Pike, pickerel, and muskie have big teeth. The best way to land pike to avoid hurting yourself or the pike is with a cradle—essentially a long, rectangular net. To land pike or muskie without a net, lift the fish by the area just in front of the tail and just in back of the pectoral fins. You can handle smaller pickerel the same way.

Big trout and bass have tiny teeth that can hurt. But they will not do much damage unless you handle them excessively. You can use the same landing method as with pike, but with trout and bass, it is a good idea to hold the lower lip at the same time you support the back of the fish just in front of the tail.

203 WADING WITH A FLOTATION VEST

A good safety device when wading is one of the new (and newly Coast Guard–accepted) SOSpenders by Landfall Navigation, or similar inflatable vests. These are simple inflatable vests that come in a variety of colors and styles. You can sometimes wear them in place of fishing vests (some have pockets) or with any other fishing vest. They can be kept un-inflated, so as to not be intrusive, yet inflated instantly with the supplied CO_2 cartridge, or more slowly, by mouth. They are ideal when wading any large water, deep water, or where chest-high waders might be required.

202 FISHING FLIES UPSTREAM

Make your casts straight or at an angle upstream to minimize drag when dry fly or nymph fishing. This allows the fly to drift with minimal or no drag from the side currents, although it is necessary to keep the line snug without pulling on the fly. If nymph fishing, the easiest way to do this is with a yarn-type strike indicator that can be watched for drag or a strike. Yarn or other strike indicators also make it easier to keep unnecessary slack out of the line.

204 NIGHT FISHING

Fly fishing at night can sometimes take the biggest fish. It has its own set of thrills and advantages, but also some difficulties. If you are fishing under a bright moon and your eyes have adjusted for the dark, you can often see your casts. If fishing on a black night, pick out the fly that you will be using before dark, and do not use tandem fly rigs (too dangerous). Use a heavier leader tippet than you needed during daylight (the fish won't see as well either and the heavier tippet won't be spotted). Be sure you thoroughly know the water you are going to fish.

Make short, controlled casts in situations where the backcast will not hang up, and stay away from fishing surface structure. Wear and use a small headlamp for tying leaders or changing flies and when landing fish. Have fun, keep it simple, and don't get into areas or situations where you feel uncomfortable. For safety, always fish with a buddy.

205 READING THE WATER FOR TROUT

Trout are river and stream fish, and you have to know how to read the water to know where to cast your fly. Fish are just like people—only wetter. They like comfort and food. Trout get both by staying close to the bottom or to rocks and boulders in the stream. These spots have far less current than open midstream water, so they can rest comfortably. These spots also have food wash by continuously, so that a trout can swing out to grab a bite to eat and then return to the comfort and safety of its holding spot.

As a result, fish deep with weighted flies, fish in the white water of plunge pools where waterfalls enter a pool; fish the tails of pools; and fish in front of, in back of, and beside any rocks, ledges, or boulders in the stream. The exception to this occurs when trout are taking dry flies or on big constant-flow waters where trout hang around waterweeds for shade and comfort.

206 FISHING A FARM POND

If you are a right-handed fly caster, and fishing a farm pond from shore, work around the pond clockwise. If you are a left-handed caster, work counterclockwise. The reason is that you can keep the line closer and parallel to the bank, and hold your false casts up over the water rather than over brush or grass. You can work your flies or bug easier this way, since your rod hand will be closest to the water.

207 WADING ON A SANDY BOTTOM

When standing on a sandy bottom, any fast-moving current or tide washes sand out from under your feet. This can occur on a tidal flat, fly fishing the surf, fishing sandy-bottom rivers and streams, and on sandy beaches or flats. To prevent currents from digging you into a hole, or sinking you deeper into the water when you are up to your armpits in your waders, move occasionally before the sand completely erodes your position.

"What started as a passion, became a way of life. That way of life became a vocation, but remained a passion. It's led me to fantastic, exotic, fishing destinations around the world and offered me the chance to pioneer, innovate and most importantly, meet the people who have shaped the fly fishing world and my life."

—Flip Pallot

208 FISHING FLIES DOWNSTREAM

Some trout are so easily spooked that they shy away from any fly where they can see the leader, regardless of how fine the tippet is. One way to fool these fish is to cast from an upstream location, and allow the fly to drift straight downstream to them in their feeding lane. By doing this, the trout see the fly before seeing any leader and often take after a short follow. The one problem with this is that you must allow some extra time for the fish to take the fly so that you do not pull the fly straight upstream and out of the fish's mouth after it strikes.

209 CASTING UPSTREAM TO TROUT RISES

When trout rise to take an insect off the surface, they create a ring that quickly sweeps downstream. In addition, trout often drift downstream to examine a floating insect before taking it. Both of these often create false impressions as to where a trout will take a fly or first sees a fly. Make sure that you cast well upstream of where you see a trout taking insects, but make sure that the fly follows the exact insect feeding lane of the trout.

210 LEAF-HOOKED FLIES

If a fly catches on a tree leaf, you can often use your fly rod to retrieve it. For this, raise your fly rod and catch the fly by the hook with the tip-top of the rod. Then carefully pull the fly free, pulling straight on the fly rod to dislodge the fly from the leaf. Note: This can be dangerous to the rod if not done right, or if you have to pull too hard. If you have a very expensive fly rod or if the fly catches on a twig instead of a leaf, you will be better off sacrificing the fly than risking the rod.

211 CASTING ABOVE THE WATER SURFACE

Cast as if the water is 3 feet (0.9 m) higher than it really is to make a delicate presentation of a fly when trout fishing. That way, the line and leader straighten out and the fly will drift to the water surface gently, rather than slamming down hard as it might if casting to the water surface. The result can often make the difference between a trout that takes and a trout that ignores your offerings.

212 DAPPING FOR TROUT

An easy way to take trout in a small stream is to dap for them. This is a method of dropping a fly directly from the rod tip to the water, rather than casting the fly to the fish. To do this, use a long rod, 9 feet (2.7 m) or longer. For best fishing, try small streams where you can poke the rod out from the brush and drop a fly to a feeding trout. The advantage of dapping is that you can present a fly without any drag problems associated with casting since only the fly should touch the water surface.

213 TREE-HOOKED FLIES

If a fly hooks in a tree, do not pull on the tippet to pull the fly to you to remove it. Instead, try to reach any of the adjacent branches, grab the ends of them, and pull the branches down. Make sure that you grab the thickest branches to prevent breaking them and having to start over. Once you have pulled the branches down, reach out and dislodge the fly.

214 CONTROLLING THE "LAZY S" CAST

Once you get comfortable with it, there are ways to control the "lazy S" cast so that you can place the S's where you want in the line, to be washed out by the current and give you a longer drift. To make "S's" throughout the length of the cast, shake the rod through the entire final forward cast. To make S's at the end of the fly line and close to the fly, shake the rod at the beginning of the forward cast and then stop. You will get these curves in the line only on the front half of the line.

To make S's in the rear of the line, wait until the final cast is starting to straighten out and then make the side-to-side shakes to create slack in the line. Note that you can also control just how much slack you want by making either slight shakes for minimal curves, or hard side-to-side shakes for lots of curves across a fast current or for a longer drift.

215 CHUMMING ON A TROUT STREAM

Fifty years ago, the books and research of Charlie Fox and Vince Marinaro noted the importance of "chumming" in trout streams to locate trout and trout lies. They developed and fished with terrestrial patterns to imitate the inchworms, grasshoppers, leafhoppers, crickets, beetles, termites, and ants that live along a stream. Often these natural insects fall into a stream where the trout gobble them up. You can chum the same way with land insects, throwing them into the water to locate trout, finding the best feeding lane in which to throw a fly, and conditioning trout to feed. Just make sure that this practice is legal in your fishing area before trying it.

216 "LAZY S" CAST

Water in the middle of a stream runs faster than water along the sides, creating a current that pulls on the fly line to create a belly in the line and drag the fly unnaturally. To prevent this and get a longer natural drift, make a "lazy S" cast.

To do this, make a normal cast, but use a longer length of line than necessary. On the final forward cast, wiggle the rod sideways to create S's in the line as it lands. These S's take longer to wash out in the fast center current, creating more time for the fly to drift naturally.

217 SNAGS FROM DOWNSTREAM FISHING

To get un-snagged when you are hooked downstream, have a little patience. Allow slack and pay line out through the rod guides until you get a large belly in the line. This belly must extend downstream of the snag for this method to work. In many cases, the water resistance and pressure on the line belly is enough to pull the fly free.

If this does not happen automatically, wait until you get a large belly of line, stop paying out the line, hold it, and then jerk the rod strongly to the side. The result will pull on the line belly, which in turn creates downstream pressure on the fly to pull it free. It does not work all the time (nothing does) but it is a quick easy fix for many snag situations.

219 SHAKING THE ROD TO FREE SNAGS

There are several ways to get flies off of snags. One is to shake the rod lightly and very rapidly. To do this, hold the rod high so that you have a direct line from the rod tip to the fly, with no line on the water. Then shake the rod rapidly, but not hard. You don't want to break the tippet or risk the rod. What you do want is to set up a series of rapid movements of the tippet connected to the fly to jerk the fly free.

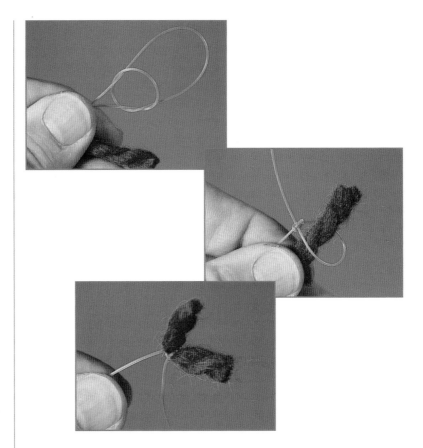

218 ATTACHING YARN STRIKE INDICATORS

Yarn strike indicators are great for nymph fishing. They are fluffy, they look like bits of nothing to trout when floating on the surface, and you can easily see them under all conditions. To use them, cut off a small piece of yarn and then make a slipknot in the leader where you want the strike indicator positions. Run the yarn through the loop formed by the slipknot and pull the knot tight. To remove the strike indicator, hold the knot end of the leader and pull on the strike indicator to create some slack in the loop. Then remove the strike indicator and straighten the leader section by pulling on it before fishing again.

"On bass: This is one of the American freshwater fishes; it is surpassed by none in boldness of biting, in fierce and violent resistance when hooked."

—W. H. Herbert (Frank Forester)

Fishes and Fishing (1850)

220 HAND-LANDING FISH

To land a fish by hand, you have to keep this slippery creature from sliding out of your hand while you get it under control for keeping or releasing. Grip the fish in back of the head with your hand around its body and your fingers in front of and behind the pectoral fins on one side. If you can turn the fish on its side or turn it over, the fish will squirm less. This upside-down position keeps a fish quiet while you remove the hook.

221 NETTING FISH

Nets are the traditional way to land fly-caught fish. Both short-handled wading and long-handled boat nets are available, in a variety of bag diameters and depths. First make sure that the fish is tired and ready to land. Lower the net into the water, and lead the fish head first into the net. Never land a fish tail first.

If the fish is moving head first into the net and strikes the net, it will dive farther into the net. If netted tail first and striking the net, it will leap out of the net. Once the fish is in the net, rapidly raise the net. If the fish tries to jump out of the net, and if you have a deep enough bag, turn the net frame sideways to close the net opening and secure the fish.

222 LANDING FISH WITH A GAFF

Anglers still use gaffs to land big fish. You can use them when you want to keep or kill a fish, or as a lip gaff when you only want to get your fly back before releasing the fish. In the former case they are necessary for big fish to prevent losing them, while lip gaffing is necessary for large fish, such as tarpon, or toothy critters, such as barracuda, pike, and bluefish.

To land a fish that you are going to keep, wait until the fish is tired. Don't try to repeatedly strike after a lively fish. With the fish along-side the boat, lower the gaff in the water, preferably over the shoulder of the fish and strike the fish a little bit back of the head. Once you gaff the fish, continue to pull up on the gaff to bring the fish into the boat and preferably drop it into a fish box or cooler.

To lip gaff a fish, bring the exhausted fish close, position the gaff directly underneath the lower lip or jaw, and bring the gaff up through the thin skin in the lower jaw. An alternative to this, practiced by some tarpon guides, is to position the gaff inside the fish's mouth, and then push the gaff down through the thin skin of the lower jaw. This allows pinning the fish by the gaff point to the underside of the gunwale to stabilize the fish and remove the fly.

223 EMERGENCY TIP-TOPS

Even if you do not carry a field tackle repair kit, it makes sense to carry a spare tip-top, along with a tube of heat-set glue, in your fly vest. That way, if you do unfortunately break a tip section of your rod, you can glue on the spare tip-top and continue fishing. Make sure that the tip-top that you carry is a size or two larger than your tip end, since breaking a tapered tip section will require a larger tube than the one mounted on the rod. Carry a few matches or a small lighter, to melt the glue, smear on the broken rod tip end, and slide the spare tip-top in place.

224 SNAGS FROM SURFACE STRUCTURE

To get free when snagged on a surface rock or log, use a modified roll cast. Keep the line loose, since you do not want to drive the hook deeper into the snag. Then raise the rod or hold it at your side for a standard roll cast or side-armed roll cast. Usually, the side-armed roll cast is easier to make and more effective. Make the roll cast loosely and the rolling line will usually pull the fly backward and off the snag. If it does not come free, try again with a more forceful roll cast.

225 REMOVING FLIES

The easiest and best way to release fish is to never take them out of the water, but remove the fly while they are tired but resting. To do this, tire the fish enough so that you can control it without touching it. Hold the leader close to the fly and work the fly out of the fish's mouth. Push the fly sharply back to disengage it. If it is a large fly, hold the body of the fly and partly lift the fish up to cause the fly to pull out. Lacking that, use pliers or hemostats to hold the fly and twist it out of the fish. Tools made exclusively for fly removal include the Ketchum Release by Waterworks, which features a small slit-sided collar on a handle. To use this, fit the slit-sided collar over the line and slide it down over the fly to push the fly back and out of the fish. Several sizes are available for freshwater and saltwater fish.

226 DRIFTING A FLY TO AN UNDERCUT BANK

One trick to get trout to hit when they are hiding under overhanging brush or an undercut bank is to drift a fly to them. Often this is impossible if snags are in the area, but there is one method that makes this easy. The trick is to pick a tree leaf from along the bank and hook your fly to the outer edge of the leaf. Use a dead, dry leaf so that it will float. Position yourself above the trout lie and pay out leader and line to drift the leaf with the current to the position of the fish. Once you are in the right area, make a quick, sharp jerk to pull the hook free of the floating leaf and allow the fly to drop into the water in front of the trout.

"That is winter steelheading: long hours of cold, interminable work, punctuated with breathless moments of excitement."

—Steve Raymond

The Year of the Angler (1973)

Chapter 7

Saltwater Fly Fishing

Reading Water, Locating Fish, Choosing Flies

227 READING SALTWATER—NATURAL STRUCTURE

Natural structure has always held fish. Good natural structure includes flats, mangrove shorelines, marsh grass areas, seaweed, channels, bays, inlets, coves, downed trees, and the like. You'll typically find snook, a tropical species, around mangroves shorelines. They often hide deep under the mangrove root system on a high tide, but move out as the tide lowers and their hidey-holes disappear. Downed trees along the shore are good for striped bass, as are overhanging marsh banks. White perch and sea trout like to school around oyster beds, while grassy areas are good for striped bass, sea trout, white perch, and snook. Learn the habits and habitat of the species you seek so you know how to find them along the structure-rich shorelines.

228 READING SALTWATER—MAN-MADE STRUCTURE

While plying the coasts for trade and recreation, people have added a lot of structure that holds inshore species, such as striped bass, weakfish, sea trout, cobia, bluefish, redfish, and similar species. Structure possibilities to try on a running tide include any man-made object, such as rock jetties, riprap, concrete bulkheads, bridge pilings, piers, sunken ships, water pipes, industrial outflow areas, dry docks, offshore oil rigs, construction sites, bridges, buoys, channel markers, lighthouses, and similar structures of concrete, rock, metal, and wood.

Realize that some structure is better for certain fish than others. For example, buoys are good for cobia, while jetties are best for stripers and sea trout. Riprap and bulkheads are good for white perch and sea bass, while offshore oil rigs are good for sharks, cobia, and reef fish, such as grouper. Flotsam in open water is sometimes good for a dolphin or two.

"...to master ocean fly fishing, nothing beats time on the water."

—Lou Tabory
Inshore Fly Fishing (1992)

229 SALTWATER FISH DANGERS

Many saltwater fish are more dangerous than freshwater fish. Dangers include teeth (barracuda, bluefish, and sharks), sharp gill plates (snook), crushers (drum, redfish, grouper), and spines (white perch, dolphin, cobia). Unless you know the species that you are catching, and know how to handle it, be especially careful of the teeth, crushers in the back of the throat, and sharp spines on any fish.

230 TWO-HANDED RETRIEVE

It is impossible to retrieve too fast for a barracuda. In fact, without a fast retrieve, 'cuda will often shun the fly. There are two ways to make a fast retrieve with fly tackle. One is to hold the rod between your upper legs after making the cast, lean over, and retrieve the fly by rapidly pulling on the fly line hand-over-hand. A second method is to grip the rod by the handle under your upper arm and retrieve the line as above with both hands. When doing this, use whichever arm is most comfortable for you.

231 BIG-GAME FLY FISHING

Big-game fly fishermen after billfish use very heavy outfits to throw very large flies. Often these flies include a large foam head to keep the fly on the surface where the billfish expect it after being teased to the boat transom with a large billfish teaser. However, hard foam heads often cause the fly to slide right out of the fish's mouth without hooking it. Many anglers are now using soft foam heads made from foam similar to that used for upholstery.

This foam absorbs water and sinks in time, but the big advantage is that it collapses when hit, thus allowing the fly to slide into the corner of the fish's mouth for a positive hook-up. Also, you are only throwing these foam-head flies when you have a fish behind the boat, and not blind casting all day where the floatability of the fly and head might be of concern.

232 BOTTOM-FEEDING FISH

Bonefish, redfish, and other shallow-water bottom feeders leave puffs of mud as they scrounge along the bottom. These puffs of mud, or marl, are keys to fish being in the area. Just realize that they are often indicators of where the fish were, not always where they are now. Also, highly dispersed puffs indicate areas where fish have left, since the dispersion of silt can only occur over a period of time. If you see puffs of marl progressing in a given direction, cast your fly ahead of the most recent puff to intercept the fish, or look for other signs (tailing, flashes of their sides, nervous water, etc.) that indicate fish in the area.

233 TIDES

Most saltwater fish move and feed more on a moving tide. A falling tide concentrates game fish at creek mouths and inlets where bait tumbles off of a flat or out of a marsh. Incoming tides concentrate fish around buoys, jetties, and other structure where they can ambush bait at high tide. Few fish move or eat on still water when the tide is dead high or low.

234 SALTWATER FLIES

Most saltwater baits come in several basic colors. Most baitfish are some shade of white, cream, black, or yellow. Thus, most popular saltwater flies come in these colors. Silversides are white and shiny; shad are cream-colored; eels are black or very dark brown; and killifish are yellowish. Exceptions to the above basic color scheme are patterns, such as those for shrimp and crabs, where tan flies are often best for tropical fishing. Tie or buy your flies in the colors that simulate the baitfish or fish food in your area.

235 POPPING AND SWAPPING

One way to catch wide-roaming fish when fly fishing from a boat is a "popping and swapping" method that is ideal for stripers, bluefish, and many tropical reef fishes. To do this, carry a large spinning outfit rigged with a chugger from which you have removed the hooks. Then one angler in the boat (or the guide) can cast and work the lure to attract fish and pull them within fly casting distance.

With the fish within casting distance, the fly caster (already rigged and prepared, of course) casts a similarly large popper to land on top of, or close to, the spinning chugger. By immediately working the fly rod popper and allowing the spinning chugger to rest, the fish will switch to the moving popper for a quick hook-up. Use this same technique when fishing from shore to bring fish to within fly casting range.

236 CHUMMING IN SALTWATER

One of the best ways to catch saltwater fish on a fly is by chumming. To do this, anchor a boat and then release a chum slick of ground baitfish and fish oil. Another alternative is to drift over a reef and suspend a chum bag off the bottom to attract fish to your deep-fished fly. There are lots of different chums available, including any ground-up mix of baitfish, clams, shrimp, and the like; cat food, prepared bagged or frozen chum, chum fish oil, etc. Often you can combine these to make a long-lasting chum. Just make sure that you grind any homemade chum fine, since the purpose of chum is to attract fish with scent, not to feed them.

237 BOGAGRIP TO LAND FISH

A BogaGrip is a sleeve-operated fish landing device with two gripping jaws (like blunt ice tongs) to hold a fish by the lower lip. It also has a spring-operated scale to weigh the fish. There are a number of substitutes available that do the same thing. These are great for landing fish that are difficult to handle, toothy, or fish that you just want to weigh before releasing.

To use these tools, first ready the fish for landing. Pull back on the slide or sleeve to open the jaws, place the grippers around the lower jaw of the fish, and allow the sleeve to close, closing the grippers on the fish. Lift and weigh, then put the fish in a fish chest or release it over the side. These are also ideal for getting a photo or two of a fish before you release it.

238 FLY FISHING UNDER DIVING BIRDS

To fish effectively under diving birds in saltwater situations, modify your casting slightly. First, make short casts that get to the fish without casting through a flock of birds. Second, with due care for others on the boat, make side casts that keep the line, leader, and fly close to the water surface to minimize high casts that might catch birds. Once you cast, lower the rod tip so that the line falls rapidly to avoid bird contact. If a bird follows your fly, allow it to sink or jerk it rapidly to keep from hooking the bird.

239 SPOTTING SALTWATER FISH

Anglers sight-fish fly rod quarries. You can spot some fish, such as bonefish, redfish, and permit, by their tails above water as they root along the bottom in shallow water. Tarpon roll on the surface, completely different from the typical moving dorsal fin of cruising sharks. You can find stripers and bluefish breaking on the surface taking bait, while you can sometimes see reef fish while they work around coral and flash in the water.

240 SPOTTING BIRDS THAT SIGNAL FISH

Gulls, pelicans, and terns are often great "bird dogs" to find fish. Use binoculars to spot them and check what they are doing. Experts consider 8X50 binoculars as the best for this. Birds signal fish activity as follows: Randomly flying birds or birds sitting on the water mean no fish. Hovering birds in a given area, yet not diving, are usually signaling deep fish or bait—neither bird nor fly can reach it. Birds actively diving are seeking bait that game fish (such as stripers, bluefish, sea trout, and similar inshore species) drove to the surface.

"Hunting and fishing are the second and third oldest professions, yet bonefishing is the only sport that I know of, except perhaps swordfishing, that combines hunting and fishing."

—Stanley M. Babson
Bonefishing (1965)

241 UNHOOKING BIRDS

When fishing under diving birds, it is almost inevitable that you will hook a bird sometime. Be gentle with the bird when unhooking it, since it is not the bird's fault that it ran into your line or fly. Also, realize that in most cases, it is a two-person operation. Reel or strip in the bird. When it is close to the boat, have your partner throw a towel over its head. That is particularly important with pelicans, as they have long, sharp bills and strong necks. You don't want to risk injury.

With the bird covered with a towel, check to see if the line/ leader is wrapped around a wing or if the bird is hooked. If the line is wrapped around the bird, unwrap it and release the bird. If the bird is hooked, hold the fly with pliers by the bend of the hook and jerk the hook out of the bird and release it. Make sure that the bird is not wrapped in other parts of the line and is completely clear of everything when you toss it into the air as you remove the towel covering.

242 WADING IN SALTWATER

Stingrays often hide in the sand, where they remain camouflaged. On tropical flats when you are wading for bonefish or permit, this can be a real danger if you step on one. To guard against this, slide your feet along the bottom rather than taking steps to lift your foot from the bottom. Sliding your foot will cause any stingray to scurry away without stabbing you.

Chapter 8

Fly Fishing From Boats

Tactics for Anchors, Drifting, Line Tangles

243 HOOKED FISH UNDER THE BOAT

If the water is deep enough, hooked fish often dive under the boat or swim under the boat to the opposite side. This can happen with any fish, but is particularly common with salt-water species. Stick the rod straight down into the water far enough for the line to clear the rough bottom and to prevent rod breakage. On a large charter boat, this might mean extending the rod into the water up to the grip. Take special care in shallow water that you do not stab the rod into the bottom and break it.

If you can't coax the fish back to your side of the boat, keep the rod tip under the water and work around to the opposite side of the boat to where you can lift the rod and resume fighting the fish. Walk the rod around the bow or stern in doing this, whichever end is easiest, and with less possibility of tangling line. If anchored from the bow, you will have to take the rod around the stern and work the line under the engine prop.

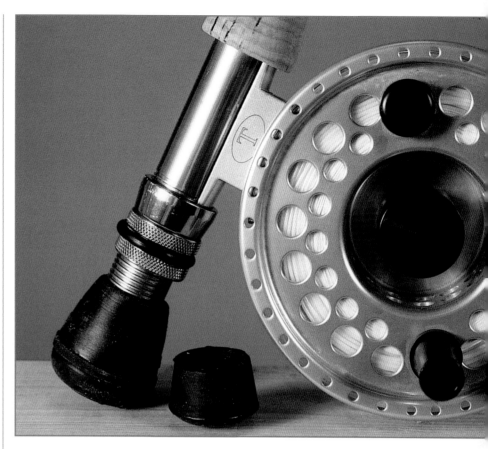

244 SLIDING RODS

Unless your rod has a short extension butt with a rubber end, your rod will likely slide when placed butt down on a boat deck while changing flies or performing other chores. To prevent this, buy a rubber (not slippery plastic!) crutch tip from a drugstore to slip onto the end of the reel seat. Up-locking reel seats are best for this, but a modified and slightly cut out crutch tip will fit on down-locking reel seats as well.

If the crutch tip is too large to fit the reel seat diameter, temporarily wrap some masking or electrical tape around the end of the reel seat until the crutch tip fits. Note that crutch tips do come in different sizes, including $7/8$- and 1-inch (2.2- and 2.5-cm) inside diameters.

"No angler merely watches nature in a passive way. He enters into its very existence."

—John Bailey

Reflections on the Water's Edge (N.D.)

245 CASTING DISTANCE

If you are boat fishing with a buddy who is new to fly fishing and who can't cast more than about 40 feet (12.2 m), it does no good to position the boat 60 feet (18.3 m) away when it is his or her turn to cast. He can't reach the fish and his attempts will only result in poor casts and frustration. If necessary for shallow-water fish, stay as low as possible with both of you crouching to reduce visibility to the fish. In most cases, it is best to stay as far as possible from a casting target, shoreline, points, structure, or feeding fish, provided that you can comfortably reach the fish and get a fly to them accurately.

246 CASTING

In a lot of fly fishing situations, there is an angler at each end of the boat, often with a guide on a poling platform at one end. A line drawn through those two or three people is usually on the boat axis. For this reason, never cast along the axis of the boat for fear of hooking your partner or the boat guide.

Except for unexpected fish that appear off the bow or stern, guides will position the boat so that the fish or casting targets are to the side where both anglers can get a shot at them. The exception to the above occurs when you have to position the boat in the direction of the cast, because of tide or currents. For these situations, check with your buddy or the guide first, make sure that they duck or are out of the way and only then make your cast. Each time you do this, check first and warn others in the boat of your intentions.

247 DUMMY CASTS

When boat sight-fishing, strip off all the line you need and then make a cast before you start searching for fish. Then strip the line back in. If you don't take this step, the line that you cast will be underneath the line just stripped from the reel and may cause a tangle or delay when you are ready to make a critical cast to a fish.

248 CLOTHING AT SEA

If fishing from a boat, wear only shirts with button-down collars. The reason is that in shirts without button-down collars, the collars can flap and abrade your face on a long run to the fishing grounds, or during high winds on any fishing trip.

249 SHIRT POCKETS

When fly fishing from a boat, you might have to lean over the gunwale to land or release a fish taken on a light tippet. Or you might want to rinse your hands after catching a fish and before handling a camera to take a photo. In any of these tasks, you can lose the contents of a shirt pocket—pens, pencils, notepads, pocket cameras, cell phones. Just as bad, even if you do not lose items, you can break them as you lean your chest against the inside of a gunwale to unhook a fish or help to release it.

Thus, remove all items from your shirt or jacket top pockets and place them in storage on the boat or in a gear bag for safekeeping.

250 PUSH TO BREAKING FISH

If you run your boat right up to a school of breaking stripers in coastal waters, the engine noise might put them down. To prevent this, consider the tide and/or wind. Stop the engine a little more than a cast length away from the school. Then let the wind or tide push your boat into the fish so that you can cast to them easily and effectively. Fished this way, the fish will not be aware of your boat or presence as they would if you were to motor into the school of fish.

251 LINE-STRIPPING BASKETS—ONE

Capt. Norm Bartlett has come up with an easy-to-make and easy-to-use boat line stripper, similar to the high-priced stripping baskets sold for the purpose. Norm buys a tall, perforated laundry basket from a discount store, adds a few bricks to the bottom for weight, and covers the bricks with indoor/outdoor carpeting to protect the fly line. These are easy to store (you might want two for two fly casters on a typical flats or center-console boat) and work well to keep line from blowing around the boat deck. Place them in the boat where needed and strip line into the tall, open-weave basket. Since these have a slight taper to them, you can store them by slipping one into the other.

252 LINE-STRIPPING BASKETS—TWO

Another easy-to-use and inexpensive boat line stripper is the fold-up spring-style leaf buckets sold in home and garden supply stores. These fold flat for storage and open instantly for use. Most are 18 inches (45.7 cm) in diameter and 24 inches (61 cm) high when in use. Manufacturers also sell these as foldable laundry baskets, so you can find them in household supplies or domestics in a general or department store.

253 ELECTRIC MOTOR CONTROLS

Electric motors are used more and more on all boats—not just bass boats where their use originated. Saltwater flats and center-console fly fishing boats use long-shaft styles. To prevent fly lines from tangling up in the foot controls, throw a large towel over the controls. Sometimes it helps to moisten the towel to prevent it from blowing around. You can still use your foot to control speed and direction, but the fly line won't catch in the control mechanisms.

254 PREVENTING LINE TANGLES—ONE

If traveling, you can't always take a line-stripping bucket and one might not be on the boat from which you fish. Instead, carry along a 6- to 8-foot-square (1.8- to 2.4-meter) net. Light nylon with mesh of about 1 to 2 inches (2.5 to 5 cm) square is ideal, as is fine-mesh minnow netting. Add pinch-on sinkers to each corner and center of the net rim to keep it from blowing around. Before stripping out your line, throw this net over any tackle. You can stand on it and fly line can't get caught around tackle boxes, reel handles, or lures. You can see tackle under the cover and reach under the net to get it.

255 PREVENTING LINE TANGLES—TWO

Slip-on "water shoes," often worn for foot protection while swimming, are ideal for fly fishing from boats. The lack of laces prevents the fly line from getting caught in them. Just be sure to wear socks with them to protect your feet and ankles from sunburn. If wading a clean flat, these also might be sufficient to provide some protection, even though they provide little ankle support.

256 PREVENTING LINE TANGLES—THREE

Use tape to cover the shoelaces, particularly the bowknot, to prevent fly lines from tangling. Duct tape is ideal for this, since it sticks well and also peels off easily at the end of the day.

257 PREVENTING LINE TANGLES—FOUR

A tip from fly rod guru Lefty Kreh is to replace your shoelaces with elastic cord, available from sewing supply stores. Run the cord through the shoelace eyelets, knot at the top with a square knot, cut off any excess and seal the knot with flexible glue. This makes it easy to open the shoe when you put them on, yet keeps the shoe in place and does not have any lace ends to tangle fly lines.

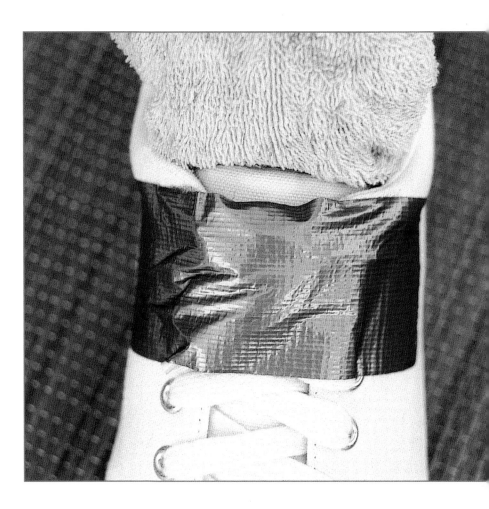

258 COVERING CLEATS

When fly fishing from boats for warm-water and saltwater species, cleats often catch fly lines. While some newer boats have retractable cleats to prevent this, most boats do not. To prevent cleats from catching fly lines, cover them completely with duct tape. This will prevent line tangles, but you can also easily remove the tape once the fishing day is over.

"It is the constant—or inconstant—change, the infinite variety in fly-fishing that binds us fast. It is impossible to grow weary of a sport that is never the same on any two days of the year."

—Theodore Gordon (1914)

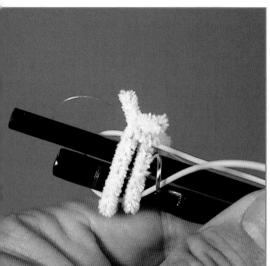

259 PROTECTING RODS—ONE

Capt. Norm Bartlett, inventor that he is, has a simple solution for protecting rods on his center-console boat. He uses closed-cell foam pipe insulation with a large inside diameter. This is usually sold in 4-foot (1.2-meter) lengths, four to a pack. This makes an ideal sleeve or soft case for a rod, ready rigged down to the fly, but broken down into its two sections. You can fold the two sections over with the line or leader, secure the ends with half of a pipe cleaner or twist tie, and slip the two sections into the case to protect the rod down to the handle.

To keep the pipe insulation from coming apart (they are partly split to be separated to fit over pipe), use a soft glue, such as Marine Goop or Pliobond, to seal the longitudinal seam. You can also glue two pieces together, end to end, make longer cases for longer rods, and then cut to length.

260 PROTECTING RODS—TWO

One way to store a ready-rigged rod in a hard case is to buy a length of 2-inch-diameter (5-cm) PVC pipe. Buy thin-wall PVC pipe, cut to length for your rod, about 56 inches (1.4 m) for a 9-foot (2.7-m) rod. Use a hacksaw to cut a long notch in one end into which the reel can slide. Smooth this notch with sandpaper and drill two small holes on each side at the end. Add a knotted loop of bungee cord through the holes. Rig the rod ready to fish right down to the fly, and then break down the rod into two pieces. Add half a pipe cleaner wrapped around the ferrule end to contain the rod sections, line and leader, and slide into the case, with the notch providing room for the reel. Use the short loop of bungee cord around the end to keep the rod from sliding out. The rod is completely protected this way, yet ready to use in seconds by removing from the case, pulling off the pipe cleaner, ferruling the rod, and casting.

261 PROTECTING REELS

One quick and simple way to protect a reel in a boat is to use an old sock. The neoprene or cloth case that usually comes with better reels is ideal, but if you don't want to risk damage to the case, the sock protects the reel, keeps the metal from damaging the gel coat on the boat, and also lessens any fish-scaring noise of the reel hitting the boat. Thick socks are best for this.

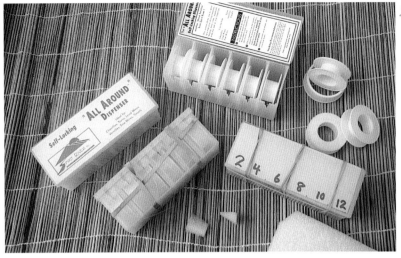

BOAT LEADER BOX

While you want a leader wallet while wading, a leader box is best for a boat. These are available commercially, but a small inexpensive one can be made from a Spirit River All Around Dispenser that has six separate compartments, each with a spool and each compartment with a slot for the leader. These are designed for fly-tying materials, but in years of tests, they work equally well for leader material. Use two rubber bands to further secure the snap lid, and one rubber band around the front to hold the leader ends. I carry two of them—one for leader materials in sizes of 2-, 4-, 6-, 8-, 10-, and 12-pound-test (0.9-, 1.8-, 2.7-, 3.6-, 4.5-, and 5.4-kg); the second for heavier leader material in sizes 15-, 20-, 25-, 40-, and 50-pound-test (6.8-, 9.1-, 11.3-, 18.1-, and 22.7-kg).

263 **ROCKING THE BOAT**

Don't rock the boat! That's good advice for boat safety, but also for fishing success. Rocking a boat unnecessarily sends out shock waves that can alert fish to your presence through their lateral line. Special nerve endings along the lateral line measure pressure waves in the water to alert fish to predators. To keep from rocking a boat, try to walk along the centerline of the boat. Walk softly rather than bouncing or walking heavily to set up boat waves. Since fly casters often cast shorter distances than those using spinning or casting tackle, and thus must be closer to the fish or quarry, this tip is particularly important.

264 **"WIND DRIFTING" A SHORELINE**

If the wind is blowing in the right direction, you can use it to blow you along a shore to fly fish bass or other lake species. To do this, determine the direction of the wind and then position your boat so that the wind carries you parallel along a shore. In lakes, and along some rivers with lots of shoreline, you can almost always find a shoreline where the wind can help you fish this way.

265 **PVC FLY ROD HOLDERS**

Fly rods are difficult to store in most small boats. One way to make simple protective holders for them is with lengths of thin-wall 2-inch (5-cm) PVC pipe, secured alongside the gunwale of the boat, with a flat support of aluminum strapping or wood to support the grip. Add bungee cord to the handle support to hold the rod grip in place while running the boat. Several of these added to any boat allow you to store rods in the same way that a sword is held in a sheath. To flare the ends of the PVC to keep from damaging guides, heat the end of the PVC pipe with a torch (do not burn it) and taper it by flaring it on a tapered glass soda bottle. Allow the pipe to cool while on the bottle so that the plastic memory does not return it to a straight pipe.

266 FISHING BAREFOOT

A big problem when boat fishing without a stripping basket is that you can step on the line on the casting deck, ruining a cast or breaking off a running fish. To prevent this, some anglers fish barefoot so that they can feel the line underfoot and clear the line before or during a cast, and when a hooked fish starts to make a run. If you do fish barefoot, just make sure to use a good sunscreen on your feet to prevent a painful burn.

267 FLY BOXES AND BAGS

Large flies, such as those used for bass, pike, and saltwater fishing will not fit into standard fly boxes. There are several good options for these when boat fishing. One is to use the clear-front, nylon-zippered pencil cases that have grommets for fitting into a three-ring school notebook. You can easily see the case contents, and even color-code these bags if you like, since a half dozen colors are available. To store them, get a sturdy, zippered, three-ring notebook, or store them in a ringed spinnerbait case, such as made by Tackle Logic, Shimano, and others. These include thin zipper-lock envelopes (although they are very lightweight) and can easily hold a dozen or more of the nylon pencil cases.

Another alternative is to use one of the large cases that have smaller, clear-vinyl front-zippered compartments designed to hold hardware lures (jigs, spinnerbaits, buzzbaits, and the like).

268 DRAG ANCHORS

When fly fishing a shallow river in a small boat, it is best to drift downstream, casting to each likely fishing spot. To slow the drift and control the boat, use a drag anchor that will not stop the boat, but which will slow the drift.

To do this, use a length of rope and 3 feet (0.9 m) of heavy chain to make a total length just short of the length of your boat. Connect the chain to the rope with a thimble and rope clamps. Use the same method at the other end of the rope to add a snap link that you can attach (when desired) to the boat bow eye or front handle.

The boat will drift stern first, and two fly casters can fish—one to each side of the boat and at right angles to the boat axis.

With this system, you can put out all or enough of the rope to slow the drift for effective fishing, while preventing the boat from turning like a top in the current. Also, if you use an outboard engine, you can leave the drag anchor out when running the boat. The short rope will never allow the prop to catch the chain.

Do not do this if you have a lot of shelf rock or other obstructions in the river. Shelf rock, or any rock or structure that can catch a chain link makes for an unsafe boating situation.

"...perhaps the greatest satisfaction on the first day of the season is the knowledge in the evening that the whole of the rest of the season is to come."

—Arthur Ransome

"The First Day at the River"

Rod and Line (1929)

269 FISHING FROM A DRIFT BOAT

Drift boat fishing is common in the West, but becoming more common throughout the country and on larger rivers. These boats are double-ended, with curved bottoms (a lot of rocker, in boatman's terminology) and designed to be held in the current for fishing by a mid-ships oarsman (the guide) positioning the boat. Many of these boats have special "leaning brackets" at each end for a fly angler to stand securely while fly casting. The easiest fishing is to follow the guide's directions and cast at right angles to the current, with the boat making a slight drift without exceeding the speed of the current. Make short casts that you can handle easily, allowing the wet flies, streamers, and nymphs to drift with the current using a sinking-tip line, and fishing dry flies with a floating line and a high rod to minimize surface drag.

Chapter 9

Care and Cleanup

Keeping Equipment in Prime Condition

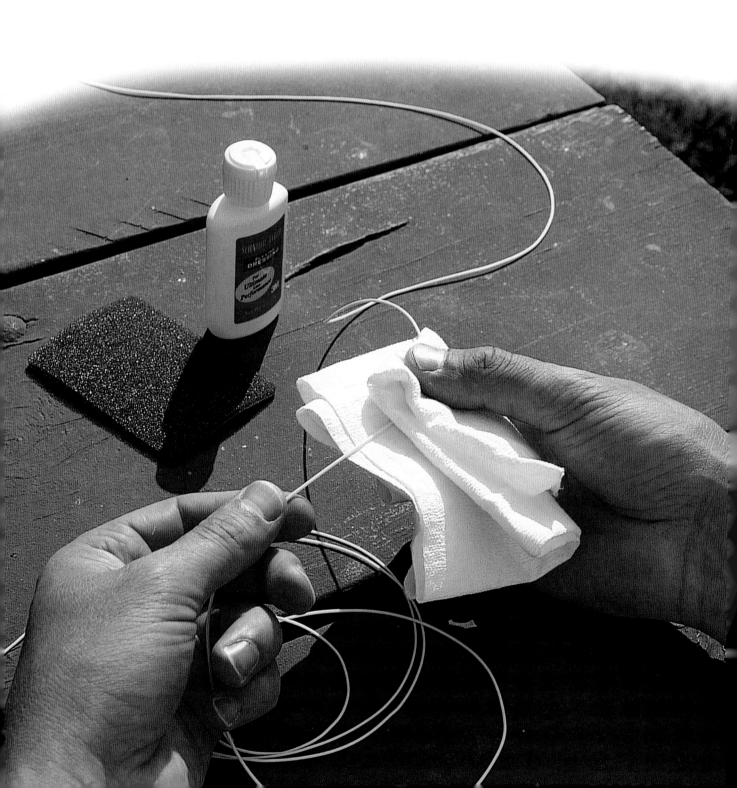

270 GUIDE DAMAGE

One easy way to check for a rough guide is to run a woman's stocking through the guide to see if the stocking will catch on any rough areas. Other products that also work include a length of fine floss or a cotton ball. On both of these, strands of fibers will come off on rough or frayed edges. These methods work for both snake guides and stripping guides.

Once you find a damaged guide, replace it with a new guide or take it to your fly shop to have it repaired. If it is not replaced, repeated fly casting can quickly ruin your expensive fly line.

271 STEAMED FLIES

By the end of your fishing season, trout flies can become pretty ratty looking and bedraggled from catching fish. The same thing can happen with any flies. To spruce them up for the next season, steam them with a teakettle. This is an old trick, often suggesting steaming flies one at a time, holding them with tweezers. To make this a simple and quick operation, put a number of flies in a tea strainer and steam them together. Just make sure that you allow all of the flies to dry thoroughly before returning them to their boxes.

"If fishing interferes with your business, give up your business...the trout do not rise in Greenwood Cemetery."

—Sparse Grey Hackle

"Murder"

Fishless Days (1954)

272 STORING FLY REELS

You can store fly reels in their cases, provided that the cases are clean, dry, and do not have any salt residue on or in them from saltwater trips. Be particularly careful of storing saltwater reels in leather cases, which absorb and hold corrosive salt. Another method is to hang up the reels from perforated board hooks, separating the reels by line size for easy selection when you go fishing.

273 STORING FLY LINES

Store your fly lines out of the heat and light. Prolonged light and heat will harm the PVC coating. You can store them safely on the reel at the end of the season, provided that the line has been cleaned and dressed, and that the line and backing are both completely dry before spooling back onto the reel.

274 STORING FLY RODS

If storing fly rods in their cases, you must make sure that the rod and the inside of the case are completely dry before casing the rod and capping the case. If unsure, case the rod and leave the cap off for moisture to dissipate. Failure to do this may result in a cased wet rod developing bubbles or the finish peeling when removed for fishing the following season. Another way to store a lot of rods is to make a wall rack where you can store them horizontally on shelves, or on overhead racks where they are out of the way and protected, yet easily available.

For a ceiling rack, make a series of looped cords on a board or lathing strip, stapling a 6-inch (15.2-cm) length of cord every 2 inches (5 cm) to make a series of loops. On a second lathing board, add a series of 1-inch (2.5-cm) cup hooks, again every 2 inches (5 cm). Then nail the boards up in the rafters. Place the two boards parallel and far enough apart so that the handle of the rod and the butt end of the tip section rest in the loop and the cup hook holds the rod ends about two-thirds up the length. Break down the rod to support all sections this way. If you have rods of different lengths (or two-, three-, and four-piece rods) adjust the two boards at an angle to each other so that they are close together at one end for short rod sections, and farther apart at the other end for longer rods and rod sections.

CARE AND CLEANUP

275 CLEANING FLY REELS

Care of your tackle requires washing that tackle after each trip, particularly when fishing in scummy or algae-filled water or around saltwater. You also have to lubricate the reel to keep it running smoothly. To keep the reel corrosion-free, remove the line annually, clean the reel thoroughly, and spray the reel with a demoisturizer, such as WD-40. This will protect the reel on future trips.

To clean your fly reel, disassemble it according to the manufacturer's instructions. In most cases, this involves nothing more than springing a lever on the axle shaft to remove the spool. If the reel is a simple click-and-pawl type, add a little grease to each tooth of the gearing. If the reel has other mechanical parts, oil or grease them according to the manufacturer's instructions. If you are unsure of how to do any of this, contact the manufacturer (write, call, or e-mail) or take the reel to a reliable fly shop for service.

276 CLEANING FLY LINE

Most fly lines come with a little pad of fly line cleaner and instructions for cleaning your fly line. If you have lost this, you can use any fly line cleaner, or get a small packet of line cleaner from your local fly shop. First stretch the line between two points, almost like a clothesline, wrapping (not tying) the two ends so as to not damage the line. Then use the cleaner on a pad or clean rag to rub the line and remove any dirt or grime. Do this several times if necessary, to remove all dirt.

Once the line is clean, "dress" it with a line conditioner to keep it slick and easy to cast. More and more companies are now making both the cleaner and dressing in one substance, so that you can accomplish cleaning and dressing with one or two wipes of the line. Once you clean and dress the line, make sure that you buff it with a dry, clean rag to remove any excess dressing and cleaner. In all cases, make sure that you do not allow other materials (demoisturizers, insect repellents, sunscreen, etc.) to come in contact with the line, as they might harm it.

"I learned how to fly fish in the hit-and-miss, trial-and-error way that makes things stick, and I learned patience, persistence, acceptance and probably a few other good things, too."

—John Gierach

Another Lousy Day in Paradise (1996)

277 WASHING REELS AND LINE

To wash fly reels, fill a sink with warm water, add a little dish detergent, and allow the reels to soak for a short time. Use an old soft-bristle toothbrush to scrub around the handles, portholes in the side plates and spool, and around the reel foot. Once the reel is clean, rinse it thoroughly and place on a towel to dry. Turn the reel over periodically to allow all water to drain. Store the reel for the next trip once it's completely dry. Separately, clean the line as described on page 111.

278 LUBRICATING FERRULES

Candle wax is ideal for lubricating and sealing ferrules on graphite-to-graphite ferrules found on virtually all current rods. Periodically, coat the male end of the ferrule with a candle stub to protect the ferrule. This will make it easy to seat and hold firmly. It also makes it easier to dismantle each time. Do not do this if you are using a metal-ferruled split-bamboo fly rod.

279 LUBRICATING METAL FERRULES

If you have a split-bamboo fly rod that has metal ferrules, you should still lubricate the ferrule to make joining and separating easy. The easiest way to do this is to rub the male ferrule lightly against the corner between your nose and your cheek. This area around your nose always has a little oil, which is just enough to lubricate the ferrule without making it so oily that it gets stuck. Never add anything such as 3-in-One oil or any other general oil to the male ferrule—you might not be able to get the rod sections apart with the suction created after joining the two ends.

280 BACKING OFF THE DRAG

Most drags designed to slow the run of fish consist of one or more hard and soft washers, similar to the brake pads and rotors on your vehicle brakes. These "soft" washers may be graphite, cork, plastic synthetics, or similar materials or combinations. To keep these washers from becoming compressed and failing the next time, back off the drag at the end of each fishing day.

281 WASHING FLY RODS

The easiest way to wash fly rods is to take them in the shower with you at the end of a fishing trip. Otherwise, wash them with a garden hose, using a sudsy wash cloth or rag to remove all grime and salt (if fished in saltwater), and use a discarded toothbrush to clean around the reel seat hoods, guide feet, and cork grip. Rinse thoroughly and allow the rod to dry. Complete, thorough drying is a must if you are going to store the rod in a closed rod tube.

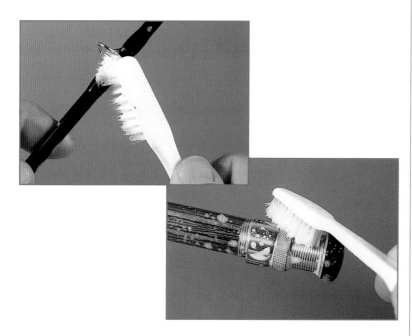

283 WASHING REELS

If you drop a fly reel or it fills with sand when you set it down on a sandbar or drop it on a mud bank, the sand, mud, or gravel can damage the reel. The best way to remove mud and dirt is to dunk the reel in the water, shake it several times to rinse it, and then pull line from the reel to remove any last remnants of gunk, gravel, or sand. If you are very careful, working in shallow water, and if your reel has a clip lever to remove the spool, you can also remove the spool when washing it. Only do this if you know that there are no loose parts to fall out. If you wash it in saltwater, be sure to thoroughly rinse and wash the reel with fresh water at the end of the day—something that you should do in any case when saltwater fishing.

282 DRYING HIP BOOTS AND WADERS

It is important to dry out your hip boots or waders after each trip. Sweat buildup can, in time, rot out the inner lining. Dry them by hanging them up and inserting a vacuum hose on "blow" into each leg until the boots dry. You can also use a hair dryer, but make sure that the hair dryer is on the "cool" or "blow only" setting, not forcing heat into the boot.

You can also fold the boots open to air dry them. To keep the boot leg open to dry, use an insert, such as the soft-foam swimming floats that are sold each summer. Do not use things such as a "tube" of wire hardware cloth, a roll of sheet metal, or a cut length of PVC tubing, since any of these might have a wire end or ragged edge that could cut the boot.

Chapter 10

Travel With Fly Tackle

On the Road & In the Air

284 TRAVEL BOOT-FOOT WADERS

Air travel is becoming increasingly difficult and increasingly confining in the amount of luggage allowed as baggage. For any travel, consider lightweight, travel-style boot-foot waders. They are lighter to carry, less cumbersome to use than the separate stocking-foot and brogue waders, and easier to pack. If fishing in a cold climate, you can insulate them by adding flannel pajama bottoms, long johns, or sweat pants under your pants.

285 ROLLING DUFFLE BAGS

Today manufacturers make many duffle bags long enough to carry travel rods. They have stiff bottoms and rollers so that you can drag them around without damage. These are ideal for travel, since you can pack your travel rods in the case and lessen the possibility of a separate rod case going astray. Just make sure that you have a long enough duffle and that the zipper opening allows you to pack the rods. For 9-foot (2.7-m) four-piece rods, you need an opening to take 29- to 30-inch (73.7- to 76.2-cm) rod cases; and for three-piece rods, you need an opening to take 39- to 40-inch (99.1- to 101.6-cm) rod cases.

286 DUFFLE BAG HANDLES

Duffle bags are ideal for carrying a lot of fishing gear on trips. Most of them have two strap handles, both of which you have to hold to carry the duffle. Unfortunately, many baggage handlers for airlines, rail, and bus lines (or even your friends unloading a vehicle) might grab just one handle and tear the handle from the heavy bag. To prevent this, buy one or two screw-type chain links, called "quick links" in hardware stores. Use these to attach the two handles. That way, even if a baggage handler grabs only one strap, the two straps can't separate to tear the bag.

287 CARS AND TACKLE—ONE

Many anglers, upon returning to the car or truck after a day of fishing, place their rods on top of the vehicle so that they don't step on the rods while they remove boots and store gear. Don't do it—unless you do it the right way. The wrong way is to place the rod on top of your car where you may forget it and drive away. Hundreds of anglers run over and lose their rods this way every year. The *right* way is to place the rod on top of your car on the driver's side with the reel facing front, and then strip off a few feet of line to hang down over the front windshield. That way, you can keep your rod protected while storing gear. The fly line on the driver's side of the windshield immediately alerts you if you have forgotten to put away your rod.

Always do this on the driver's side, in case you are ever fishing alone, since you may not see the line in front of the passenger's side. I've tried this in all sorts of fishing situations, with all colors of fly lines, and have yet to find anyone who does not see the line and who drives off with the rod on top of the car.

288 CARS AND TACKLE—TWO

Another way to protect the rod after a trip is to carry a square, about 18x18 inches (45.7x45.7 cm), of the rubberized sheeting used in kitchen cabinets. Lay this square on the front hood of the car. Then you can place the rods, reel down, on the square of cabinet sheeting, with the rod extending up over the windshield.

The rubberized sheet protects the car from tackle damage and protects the reel and rod while keeping them from sliding on the slick hood. The sheet rolls up easily. I glue one side to a dowel and roll it up to slip into a thin-wall, 2-inch-diameter (5-cm) PVC tube, stored on the floor by the driver's seat.

An alternative to this if your car hood is of a shape to allow it, is to set your rod with reel on the ground and prop the rod against the front hood of the car. The danger with this comes at night or when parking in wooded areas, where you might not see the dark rod against the background of trees and twigs. That way you still might run over it when leaving without realizing that the rod is there.

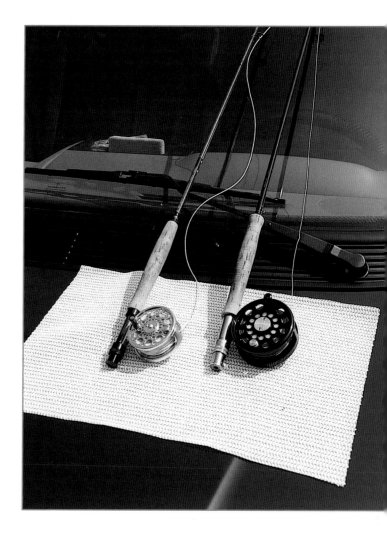

289 ROD STORAGE IN VEHICLES

The best way to travel with rods in a car is to keep them in their rod tubes, storing them carefully in the trunk or on the back seat. If you do not use, or do not have, rod tubes, bundle the rods together and store them on top of other gear so that they are not broken.

If moving while fishing, reel in excess line, break down the rods into two sections, and lay carefully on top of other gear. Many anglers break down rigged two-piece rods into two sections for travel in cars and to carry in boats. Usually these rods are completely rigged down to the fly and ready to cast once reassembled.

Capt. Norm Bartlett came up with a neat way to keep the two sections together to reduce tangles and possible damage. He uses the small spring-type hair clips to hold the rod parts together. He uses two of these, one on each end of the rod (but above the grip). These go on and come off instantly and are easy to use. They are also available in a variety of sizes to fit your individual needs. Get a bright color so they won't get lost.

Other possibilities are to use a rubber band, plastic bag twist ties or pipe cleaner to hold the sections and the line together to make it easy to assemble once at a new fishing spot. Another alternative is to use one of the car-top rack systems that are available now.

290 AIRLINE SECURITY AND FISHING TACKLE—ONE

Because of terrorist threats and security scares, things have gotten very tight at airport security screening areas. The problem arises with what to do with fly tackle. Recent stories have indicated that security has prevented passengers from taking flies on board (even small 18s and 22s), any sort of fish grip (BogaGrip or the like), hook hones, pliers, hand gaffs, and pack rods. One passenger was allowed to carry his fly reels, but forced to remove the fly lines and leave them behind for fear that he might use them as a weapon for strangling someone!

Another passenger planned to see if he could carry some travel rods on a plane, and if not, check them. The problem is that the person at the ticket counter might okay this, but someone at the security area might not allow you to pass with your rods. Then you have to go back to the ticket counter, wait in line, check your rods, and go through security again.

Even if you do get the pack rods (or any other gear) on the plane, you can have trouble with a connecting flight during a random gate check. If you had gear pass through the first flight security area, but have it disallowed on a connecting flight gate, you may have to go back to the ticket counter, perhaps pay extra to have it checked for the connecting flight, and then go back through security. You could miss your connecting flight, even if your luggage makes it to the destination.

291 AIRLINE SECURITY AND FISHING TACKLE—TWO

The fears are real and the security reactions are designed to protect us. The simplest solution is to not carry or try to carry aboard an airplane any fishing tackle. Also, consider the following suggestions:

- Pack all gear in suitcases or duffle bags. Rolling duffle bags are ideal for this, provided that they are the long style that will hold a rod case (or cases) for a 3- or 4-piece 9-foot (2.7-meter) fly rod.

- Pack reels in padded reel bags.

- If you do not have protective reel bags, use a thick sock or layer of underwear.

- Layer fly boxes and other accessories so that they are padded by clothing.

- Fold travel waders, boot-foot-style or stocking-style (your choice), and place them at one end of the duffle bag for extra padding and protection.

- Empty your fishing vest to make it simpler and less bulky to pack, and store at the other end of the duffle bag.

- Store items such as fishing knives, pliers, hook hones, disgorgers, hemostats, gaffs, thermometers, screwdrivers, wading staffs, etc., in one place or preferably in one bag or container so that inspecting federal Transportation Security Administration (TSA) security agents can find these items.

- Similarly, keep all fly boxes in one area so that agents can find and check the hook contents of the boxes.

- Store all liquids, such as fly floatants, leader sinks, insect lotions and sprays, sunscreen, etc., in two (one inside the other) zipper-seal plastic bags for safekeeping. Use sealed bags to prevent damage to luggage contents should one of the items leak.

292 AIRLINE SECURITY AND FISHING TACKLE—THREE

There are some things that you should carry onto the plane in your carry-on luggage. These include cameras, video cameras, computers, film, personal items, medical items, and prescriptions. Here are a few specific suggestions:

- Carry your camera or video equipment in a soft or hard case. If you are using film cameras, remove all film from the camera and carry the film separately. Allow the camera to go through the X-ray screening equipment without the film. The X-ray or explosives checks will not harm the camera or other equipment.

- Ask for a hand check of all film. Point out that you have several flights and that you do not want the cumulative effects of X-rays damaging your important vacation shots. At this writing, TSA personnel are cooperating and making this relatively easy.

- To make it easy for the federal TSA agents to check film, remove all film from the cardboard boxes, remove it from the plastic canister (35 mm), and carry it in a clear plastic box or a zipper-sealed plastic bag. TSA agents may run a pad over the bag (and perhaps each film can) with a small device to check for explosives, but this will not harm the film.

- For digital cameras and video equipment, allow the security agents to X-ray the entire bag of camera equipment, including the video tapes and the memory cards/discs/sticks that digital still cameras use. The X-rays will not harm any of this equipment or picture storage systems.

- Never place film or delicate camera equipment in checked luggage. The concentrated X-rays sometimes used to check equipment will damage all film, and delicate equipment can be subject to rough handling and damage for which the airline is not responsible.

- Carry medical devices and prescriptions in their original cases (pill bottle for prescriptions) so that TSA agents know that they are prescriptions and not something that you should not carry on a plane.

"There don't have to be a thousand fish in a river; let me locate a good one and I'll get a thousand dreams out of him before I catch him—and, if I catch him, I'll turn him loose."

—Jim Deren, Proprietor
Angler's Roost

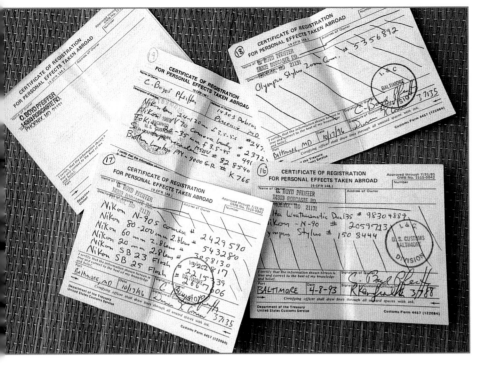

293 LUGGAGE LOCKS

Small, 4-inch-long (10.2-cm) cable ties (available from most hardware, boating, and electronics stores) are ideal as locks for luggage. You can slip them on any zippered compartment, they are inexpensive, and they do not require carrying separate keys to open each lock. If flying, make sure that you do not attach them until the airline security is finished checking your luggage. Also, make sure that you have extras for the flight home and in case security opens bags before reaching your destination. Since you can no longer carry a nail clipper on your person during air travel, make sure that someone at the other end has clippers or a pocketknife to open these disposable cable ties.

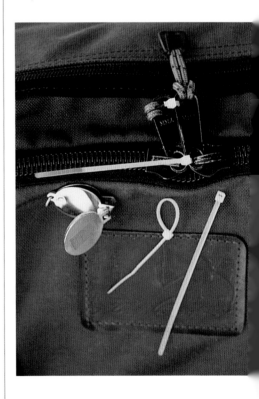

294 CUSTOMS SLIPS

If you buy products outside of the country, you may only bring back a certain dollar value before officials charge a tariff. Since many cameras, videos cameras, lap tops, electronics, palm pilots, and even some fishing tackle is made in other countries, it pays to get customs slips of all this equipment before leaving the country. Take all your foreign-made equipment to the nearest Customs office and fill out the paperwork for each piece of equipment.

Each slip requires that you supply your name, address, and the name and serial number of each piece of equipment. Usually, you can list up to about six pieces of equipment on each slip, depending upon how large you write. The Customs officers on duty will check the serial numbers on your slip against your equipment, and then mark each slip with an official Customs stamp. The good news is that once you do this, these slips are good for life. Just be sure to take all of them with you on any trip out of the country.

295 CONTROLLING TRAVEL EXPENSES

If two or more of you are going on a fly fishing trip together, make it easy by pooling common expenses, such as tolls, gas, tips, shared motel rooms, and even meals if the meals for each are about the same cost. Appoint one person "treasurer" to pay all common expenses. Then each person adds to a kitty a set amount for paying these expenses. When the fund is low, each person adds more money to rebuild it. After the trip is over, redistribute the excess money to all. A nice touch, if traveling by car, is to leave in some extra money for the vehicle owner for an oil change, car wash, etc. Keep all the money and receipts for expenses in a bag. A child's zippered pencil case or similar sturdy bag is ideal for this.

296 PHOTOCOPY YOUR PASSPORT

If traveling to a foreign country, make one or two photocopies of your passport. That way, should your passport get lost or stolen you will at least have a copy of the front page with the passport number and other vital information for getting a new passport or help from embassies, custom offices, or US consulate offices. Make sure that you keep all such copies safely secured, and in a different location than the location of your passport. Realize that this could change with Homeland Security regulations, so check first, and if not allowed for any reason, at least write down your passport number.

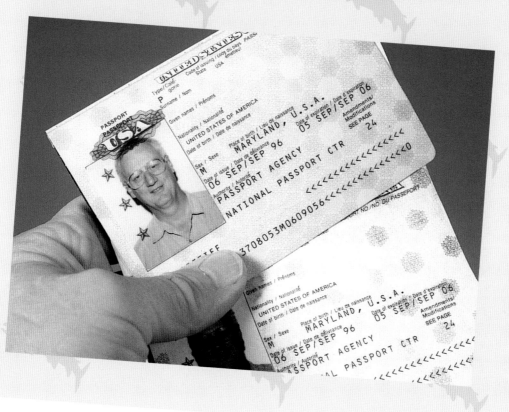

297 PHOTOCOPYING VALUABLES

If you are traveling, consider minimizing the number of credit cards that you carry to prevent problems should they be lost or stolen. Also, make a photocopy of all credit cards that you carry, making sure that the credit card numbers are visible. In addition, write down on this copy the US or international phone numbers for reporting lost or stolen credit cards to the credit card company to prevent fraudulent use. Be sure that you keep this list separate from your wallet, but in a safe place where thieves will not find it. In addition, consider photocopying any other cards that you might need while on your trip. Possibilities include health insurance cards, car registration, voter's registration cards, visas, etc.

298 **FIELD KITS**

If going on a long trip or international fishing expedition, consider carrying a field emergency kit. You will only need one for your party (everyone does not need to bring everything). You can customize such a kit for your needs. My kit fits into a six-compartment lure box, and contains the following:

- Small screwdriver set
- Small-handled socket wrench set
- Cigarette lighter
- Spare scissors
- Small pocket flashlight with fresh batteries
- Rubber bands
- Candle stub (to lubricate rod ferrules or to use as light, or to start an emergency fire)

- Small wire cutters
- Small pocket folding tool kit
- Extension butts for rods
- Nail clipper
- Spare folding pocketknife
- Spare hook hone/file
- Pipe cleaners (for securing rod sections and cleaning small parts)

Make up your own field kit as desired, based on your needs and fishing tackle, using the above as a guide. If flying, realize that even with checked baggage, you might have to remove some items, such as the cigarette lighter. Check with the airline first.

TRAVEL WITH FLY TACKLE

299 TRAVEL RODS

Even though they are a little more expensive and less readily available than standard two-piece rods, more and more fly anglers are buying all of their rods in three- or four-piece travel styles. This makes packing and storing rods easier, particularly when traveling by plane to distant fishing locations. If you travel a lot to fish, consider this, or consider adding a stock of travel rods to your tackle inventory.

300 TRAVEL NIGHT LIGHT

Often traveling fly anglers find themselves in a variety of different motels or fishing lodges. And sometimes you have to get up at night to go to the bathroom. Carry a small night light in your toiletry kit and plug it into a bathroom socket. To keep from leaving it on the last morning of your trip, write out the word "LIGHT" on a business card and place it on the sink counter. You are sure to see it and grab the light before you leave in the morning.

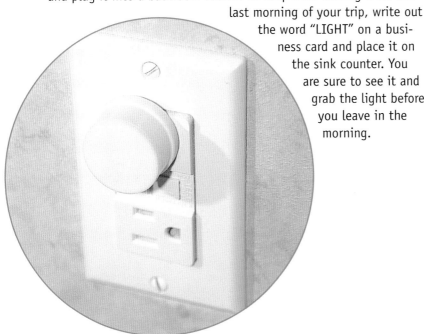

"About ninety in a hundred fancy themselves anglers. About one in a hundred is an angler."

—Col. Peter Hawker

Instructions to Young Sportsmen (1814)

Afterword

Angling ethics, as with any ethics in life, involve the golden rule—do unto others as you would have them do unto you. Thus:

- Don't crowd other anglers.

- Don't try to "steal" a spot from another fly fisherman.

- Ask anglers sitting on the bank (they might just be resting before resuming fishing) if they are fishing and if they mind if you try.

- Don't run close to another angler when boat fishing.

- Always close gates or leave a farm as you find it (if granted the right to fish).

- Don't cut through farm fields or growing crops.

- Never enter private property without permission.

- Carry out your fishing waste (line, leader tippets, damaged flies, wrappers, and containers).

- Keep only the fish that you can use if not practicing catch-and-release.

These are only a few of the commonsense "rules" of fly fishing, which revolve around respect for your fellow anglers, respect for private or public property, respect for the environment, and respect for the fish.

Remember that without water and the habitat for fish to live, we will not have any fly fishing in the future. Let's make sure that on all trips we release fish where we can, take only those we can use for one meal, and handle all fish gently.

In addition, we have to make sure that we do not litter.

Littering on the water messes up the home where fish live and makes it an unsightly place to fish.

A good way to practice a conservation lifestyle is to join a fishing club. It can provide access and introduction to fellow fly fishers, have information on local streams and possible fishing water, know about the hatches and hatch schedules, can help with a vexing fly tying or fly casting problem, and have interesting programs and speakers at their monthly meetings. You can find out more about local clubs by contacting your local library or checking with one of these two national organizations: The Federation of Fly Fishers, PO Box 1595, Bozeman, MT 59771 (406-585-7592;www.fedflyfishers.org); Trout Unlimited, 1500 Wilson Ave., Suite 310, Arlington, VA 22209-2904 (800-834-2419; www.tu.org).

Finally, the best and last tip of this book comes from my wife Brenda, a beginning fly angler who has in our few years of marriage caught on the fly bonefish, smallmouth bass, shad, trout, panfish, stripers, bluefish, and other species. Her advice is to relax and enjoy fly fishing. Great advice. Fly fishing is not, and is not supposed to be, work. Enjoy the trip. Enjoy the day. Enjoy the scenery, your companions, your catches, your challenges. And you don't have to keep the fly in the water or the rod in the air all the time. If you feel like taking a break, trying something different, watching the birds, taking a nap, eating a sandwich, watching turtles, it is all a part of the fishing experience.

Enjoy! Brenda says it's okay.

Further Reading

Borger, Gary. *Presentation,* Wausau, WI, Tomorrow River Press, 1995, 319 pages.

Earnhardt, Tom. *Fly Fishing the Tidewaters,* New York, NY, Lyons & Burford, 1995, 179 pages.

Humphreys, Joe. *Joe Humphreys's Trout Tactics,* Mechanicsburg, PA, Stackpole Books, 1981, 256 pages.

Jaworowski, Ed. *The Cast,* Mechanicsburg, PA, Stackpole Books, 1992, 222 pages.

Kreh. Lefty. *Lefty Kreh's Ultimate Guide to Fly Fishing,* New York, NY, The Lyons Press, 2003, 405 pages.

—. *Advanced Fly Fishing Techniques,* New York, NY, The Lyons Press, 2002, 248 pages.

—. *Presenting the Fly,* New York, NY, The Lyons Press, 1999, 352 pages.

—. *Fly Fishing In Salt Water,* New York, NY, The Lyons Press, 1997, 321 pages.

—. *Fly Casting With Lefty Kreh,* Philadelphia, PA, J. B. Lippincott Company, 1974, 127 pages.

Meck, Charles. *Patterns, Hatches, Tactics and Trout,* Williamsport, PA, Vivid Publishing, 1995, 338 pages.

—. *Fishing Small Streams With a Fly Rod, Woodstock,* VT, The Countryman Press, 1991, 196 pages.

Merwin, John. *Fly Fishing, a Trailside Guide,* New York, NY, W. W. Norton & Co., 1996, 192 pages.

Mitchell, Ed. *Fly Rodding the Coast,* Mechanicsburg, PA, Stackpole Books, 1995, 322 pages.

Murray, Harry. *Fly Fishing for Smallmouth Bass,* New York, NY, The Lyons Press, 1989, 190 pages.

Pfeiffer, C. Boyd. *Shad Fishing,* Mechanicsburg, PA, Stackpole Books, 2002, 226 pages.

—. *Fly Fishing—Saltwater Basics,* Mechanicsburg, PA, Stackpole Books, 1999, 232 pages.

—. *Fly Fishing—Bass Basics,* Mechanicsburg, PA, Stackpole Books, 1997, 168 pages.

Reynolds, Barry and Berryman, John. *Pike On the Fly,* Boulder, CO, Johnson Books, 1993, 166 pages.

Reynolds, Barry, Befus, Brad and Berryman, John. *Carp on the Fly,* Boulder, CO, Johnson Books, 1997, 155 pages.

Sosin, Mark and Kreh, Lefty. *Practical Fishing Knots,* II, New York, NY, Lyons & Burford, 1991, 139 pages.

Tabory, Lou. *Inshore Fly Fishing,* New York, NY, The Lyons Press, 1992, 312 pages.

Whitlock, Dave. *L. L. Bean Fly Fishing for Bass Handbook,* New York, NY, The Lyons Press, 1988, 157 pages.

Wulff, Joan. *Joan Wulff's Fly Casting Techniques,* New York, NY, Nick Lyons Books, 1987, 243 pages.

INDEX

Creative Publishing international
is your complete source of How-to information for the Outdoors.

Available Outdoor Titles:

Hunting Books
- Advanced Turkey Hunting
- Advanced Whitetail Hunting
- Bowhunting Equipment & Skills
- The Complete Guide to Hunting
- Dog Training
- Duck Hunting
- Elk Hunting
- Hunting Record-Book Bucks
- Mule Deer Hunting
- Muzzleloading
- Pronghorn Hunting
- Whitetail Hunting
- Whitetail Techniques & Tactics
- Wild Turkey

Fishing Books
- Advanced Bass Fishing
- The Art of Freshwater Fishing
- The Complete Guide to
  Freshwater Fishing
- Fishing for Catfish
- Fishing Rivers & Streams

- Fishing Tips & Tricks
- Fishing with Artificial Lures
- Inshore Salt Water Fishing
- Kids Gone Fishin'
- Largemouth Bass
- Live Bait Fishing
- Modern Methods of Ice Fishing
- Northern Pike & Muskie
- Offshore Salt Water Fishing
- Panfish
- Salt Water Fishing Tactics
- Smallmouth Bass
- Striped Bass Fishing: Salt Water
  Strategies
- Successful Walleye Fishing
- Trout
- Ultralight Fishing

Fly Fishing Books
- The Art of Fly Tying
- The Art of Fly Tying – CD ROM
- Fishing Dry Flies – Surface
  Presentations for Trout in Streams

- Fishing Nymphs, Wet Flies &
  Streamers – Subsurface Techniques
  for Trout in Streams
- Fly-Fishing Equipment & Skills
- Fly Fishing for Beginners
- Fly Fishing for Trout in Streams
- Fly-Tying Techniques & Patterns

Cookbooks
- America's Favorite Fish Recipes
- America's Favorite Wild Game Recipes
- Babe & Kris Winkelman's
  Great Fish & Game Recipes
- Backyard Grilling
- Cooking Wild in Kate's Camp
- Cooking Wild in Kate's Kitchen
- Dressing & Cooking Wild Game
- Game Bird Cookery
- The New Cleaning & Cooking Fish
- Preparing Fish & Wild Game
- The Saltwater Cookbook
- Venison Cookery

To purchase these or other Creative Publishing international titles,
contact your local bookseller, or visit our website at
www.creativepub.com

The Complete
FLY FISHERMAN ™